BOBBY BOWDEN
WIN BY WIN

BOBBY BOWDEN
WIN BY WIN

RAY G. SCHNEIDER AND PAUL M. PEDERSEN
FEATURING THE PHOTOGRAPHY OF ROSS OBLEY

ARCADIA

Published by Arcadia Publishing
an imprint of Tempus Publishing Inc.
Charleston SC, Chicago, Portsmouth NH, San Francisco

Printed in Great Britain

Library of Congress Catalog Card Number: 2003106550

For all general information contact Arcadia Publishing at:
Telephone 843-853-2070
Fax 843-853-0044
E-Mail sales@arcadiapublishing.com
For customer service and orders:
Toll-Free 1-888-313-2665

Visit us on the Internet at http://www.arcadiapublishing.com

Dedication

To Janet and Taylor—my teammates for life. R.G.S.

To my heroes—Jennifer, Hallie, Zack, and Brock. Colossians 3:17. P.M.P.

To the hard-working student-athletes who proudly represented their universities

while succeeding in earning their college degrees. R.P.O.

CONTENTS

ACKNOWLEDGMENTS

Many thanks to the numerous people from South Georgia College, Samford University, West Virginia University, and Florida State University who provided information and assistance with this book. Special appreciation goes out to the FSU Athletic Department, including Dave Hart and Pam Overton. Rob Wilson deserves special recognition for allowing us tremendous access to various materials. Lynn Hobby was also extremely helpful in responding to our many needs. Michael Morrell assisted us with our research late into the night when we're sure he could have been doing something more exciting. We're also indebted to Tina Thomas, Jeff Purinton, Chuck Walsh, and Eliot Finebloom. The media guides that these individuals produced were very helpful.

This project could not have been accomplished without help from the writings of some of the best sportswriters in the business. While a host of talented scribes provided materials used in the compilation of this book, select writers whose words had a specific impact on its content include such notables as Bill McGrotha, Steve Ellis, Bob Thomas, Bill Vilona, Doug Carlson, Kerry Dunning, Jim Henry, Brian Landman, Brent Kallestad, and Tom D'Angelo. While we researched numerous sources, some of the most important to the development of this book were the many books written about FSU and Bowden, the media guides produced by the sports information directors (most importantly those compiled by Wilson, and his predecessor, Wayne Hogan), the newspapers that regularly covered Bowden's teams, the college newspapers, the local school sports publications (most helpful was the *Osceola* and the writings of Jerry Kutz, Daniel Mitchell, Jim Lamar, Ira Schoffel, Gene Williams, and a host of other insiders), university annuals and yearbooks, publications by the Seminole Boosters, press releases, and interviews.

Other individuals who deserve much credit with various phases of this project are our publisher, Katie White, and our friend and advisor, Craig Vandegrift. Special appreciation also goes to Marian Schneider for the endless hours she spent analyzing draft after draft.

Thanks to all the players who we've taught in class, talked with on many occasions, interviewed, and photographed throughout the years. Much appreciated is Gene Deckerhoff's willingness to take time away during an off-season project with Burt Reynolds to write the foreword. Staci Wilkshire, Bowden's assistant, also deserves thanks for the patience she had in taking our repeated inquiries. Most importantly, thanks to Coach Bowden. His support and letters of encouragement for our book made the entire process worthwhile both professionally and personally.

FOREWORD

It was mid-June in 1989 and I had been offered the opportunity to broadcast radio play-by-play for the Tampa Bay Buccaneers. The Buccaneer Radio Network knew that I had responsibilities to the Florida State Seminole Radio Network, and was willing to work around that schedule and get me to my NFL assignment on Sunday, despite the additional expense. One problem. I also hosted the *Bobby Bowden Television Show* and served as the executive producer of the program. We always taped the show at 6:30 a.m. on Sunday mornings at WCTV in Tallahassee. I needed to get Coach Bowden to agree to tape his program right after the games in order to do both a college broadcast on Saturday and an NFL game on Sunday. I was in Tampa and Bobby was in Jacksonville taping a television commercial for one of our program sponsors. He was supposed to be back in Tallahassee by 4:00 p.m. I called his home around 4:30 p.m. Ann Bowden answered and said Bobby had not returned from his trip. I told her I would call back. Several phone calls later Bobby still wasn't home, and it was already 7:45 p.m. Ann was worried. So was I. As Ann and I were talking she heard someone at the door. It was Bobby. He had left for Jacksonville at 7:00 a.m. that morning and was just getting home. It had been almost 13 hours—to do one television commercial! He was not in the best of moods. The production had not gone smoothly. The production company wasn't ready. The cast hadn't arrived on time. They didn't roll tape until after 2:00 p.m. I had told Bobby he would be done and back home by 3:00 p.m. at the latest!!! Then he asked me what I needed. I told him I had a chance to broadcast NFL football. He told me he thought that was great, but why did I have to ask him about it. I told him it would involve taping his television show right after Seminole games on Saturday night, and after road games, we could be doing the show at some pretty weird times. Coach didn't hesitate in his response. "Gene," he said, "you just come pick me up and we'll do it whenever we have to. Just keep me awake."

That was 14 years ago. I'll never forget his response. Two National Championships and a Super Bowl title later, I'm still broadcasting Florida State football games on Saturday and Tampa Bay Buccaneer games on Sunday. Bobby and I are still taping the *Bobby Bowden Television Show*, more often than not, in the wee hours of the night. He has never complained. That gives you an idea of what kind of guy Bobby Bowden is. Can you imagine any other coach in any sport agreeing to work around his radio announcer's schedule? I don't think so. Bobby's record on the field speaks for itself. Those of us who know him and work with him have to tell you the rest about the best coach ever. I think you'll get an even better idea with this book.

Gene Deckerhoff
"Voice of the Seminoles"

INTRODUCTION
THE LEGENDARY BOBBY BOWDEN

Robert Clecker Bowden's arrival to the college football coaching profession ran far under the news radar screen in 1959. Anyone would have had trouble grabbing headlines—let alone an under-sized 29-year-old rookie coach from Alabama—in a year that included such major stories as Castro's rise to leadership, the plane crash claiming the lives of Buddy Holly, the Big Bopper, and Ritchie Valens, the arrival of Alaska, Hawaii, and the Chevy Corvair, and the first running of the Daytona 500.

While Bowden's "official" entrance (he had previously coached at a two-year institution—South Georgia College—where he picked up 22 wins and coach-of-the-year honors in 1955 and 1957) was not much of a newsworthy item that year, it should have been, as it marked the beginning of one of the most storied, influential, and victories coaching careers in American college football history.

During Coach Bowden's illustrious coaching span, thousands of college football coaches have come and gone. Hundreds of unforgettable gridiron leaders have entered and exited

Bowden played for the University of Alabama his freshman year before transferring to Howard College (now Samford University) where he starred as quarterback until his graduation in 1953.

the coaching profession since he won his first official game on September 19, 1959. Included in this list of coaching icons are names such as Tom Osborne, Hayden Fry, Barry Switzer, LaVell Edwards, Bo Schembechler, Vince Dooley, and Jimmy Johnson. These men were coaching greats, but not one came close to collecting the number of victories accumulated by the legendary Tallahassee field general. Bowden built a resume of winning that his coaching contemporaries and legendary forefathers could not match. Geniuses—including his coaching idols Paul "Bear" Bryant, Knute Rockne, Bob Neyland, Frank Leahy, Darrell Royal, Frank Broyles, Bobby Dodd, Bud Wilkinson, and Woody Hayes—failed to win as often as Bobby Bowden.

Bowden—who has coached thousands of players ranging from the most overachieving (Bobby Jackson) to the most talented (Deion Sanders)—has been a winner in the regular season and postseason. Of the more than 25,000 head coaches in the history of college football, Bowden is second among Division I-A coaches in all-time wins (behind Joe Paterno) in 37 years at Howard College (renamed Samford University in 1965), West Virginia University, and Florida State University (FSU). During one stretch in his career at FSU, he tallied 14 years of winning 10 or more games. His record in the postseason and big-time games is even more impressive. Bowden has the highest bowl-winning percentage (.720) of all time and the second most bowl victories with 18. His teams, from the late 1980s through 2000, established an NCAA record of 14 straight Top-Five finishes. Bowden's Seminoles played for the national championship five times over an eight-year period, winning two crowns—the last capping off an undefeated season with an unprecedented wire-to-wire ranking of number one. In addition to his success on the sideline, what Bowden represents "off the playing field cannot be measured," notes FSU Sports Information Director Rob Wilson. "Respect, class, honesty, charisma, charm, and humor; just a few of the words that describe and define this man better than wins, losses, or coaching records."

Bobby Bowden is clearly a coaching treasure and an American sports legend, even though it is sometimes hard for him to see himself that way. "To be honest," Bowden once said in typical humility, "it doesn't really feel like I should be there [among the coaching elite]." But lest anyone be mistaken, he belongs at the top of the list. Bowden has outlasted and outwon his coaching colleagues. Across six decades at football's highest and most intense level, he has excelled with a coaching style that is unique, consistent, exciting, and above reproach. Bowden crafted his special philosophy of coaching through years of dedication, exploration, and observation. He traveled to Tuscaloosa during his early coaching years to absorb as much as possible from Alabama's Frank Thomas and Paul Bryant. From "Bear," he picked up his attention to detail, organizational skills, and approach to discipline. Bowden's chicanery and flamboyance can be traced to General Neyland, who, according to Bowden, "was one of the first to bring fun into the game." But regardless of whom he patterned his game after or where he developed certain characteristics, his special blend of Southern charm and brilliant leadership is completely original and will never be duplicated. The same can be said for each of his wins. From the first unnoticed victory in 1959 through the last triumph over the rival Florida Gators attended by tens-of-thousands and covered by a media throng, this is the account of how he did it, win by win.

Known as one of college football's most media friendly coaches, Bowden has always been accessible and jovial to those wanting to talk with him.

PART I

THE LEGEND BEGINS

HOWARD COLLEGE (1959–1962)
WINS 1–31

YEAR ONE: THE 1959 SEASON (9–1)

Win No. 1
Howard 14, Maryville 0
September 19, 1959
1959 Season: 1-0

Maryville's Honaker Field—tucked away 255 miles from Birmingham, in the mountains of Tennessee—provided the setting for Bobby Bowden's first official head coaching victory. Bowden, who had been head coach the previous four seasons at a two-year college (South Georgia) shortly after receiving his master's degree from George Peabody College, quickly established himself at Howard as a play-calling gambler, using trickery (or "crowd pleasers" as Bowden calls them) to account for all the scoring in his first win. As Bowden noted to reporters years later, he "does not want to play a game without something up his sleeve." After a scoreless first quarter, Bowden took the first risk of his coaching career—resulting in the first points a Bowden-coached team ever scored. Quarterback Joe Milazzo completed a short pass to Don Coleman. The receiver then pitched the ball to Buddy Bozeman, who ran the remaining 36 yards for a touchdown. The third quarter also saw the creative side of Bowden as halfback George Versprille—a junior college All-American at

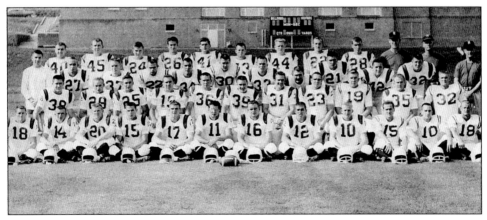

The 1959 Howard Bulldogs gave Bowden (third row, far right) his first victory.

South Georgia who transferred to Howard with 15 other teammates in order to join Bowden—took a reverse and scampered 54 yards for a touchdown. As would become a staple of teams under Bowden's direction, the defense played a big part of this historic victory, limiting the Scotties to 23 rushing yards and 65 total yards of offense. The defense even helped put the final two points on the scoreboard in the fourth quarter when Don Wiginton blocked a punt that bounced out of the end zone for a safety. Benny Storie—the only player on scholarship when Bowden arrived at Howard—led the team with 18 solo tackles. Little did the fewer than 200 spectators attending the game know that they had just witnessed the first win of a coaching legend.

Win No. 2
Howard 20, Sewanee 0
September 25, 1959
1959 Season: 2-0

On paper, this game appeared to be a mismatch. Sewanee was riding a 14-game winning streak and Howard—although 1-0 to begin the 1959 season—had only one victory in 1958. Bowden, facing his second straight road contest in Tennessee, had his players believing they could beat anyone and used a total team effort to shut out the Tigers. After being held scoreless in the opening quarter for the second straight game, the Bulldogs opened the scoring in the second quarter when Bozeman leaped high for an 18-yard touchdown pass from Milazzo. Time-consuming drives of 71 and 63 yards accounted for Howard's final tallies. Milazzo—whom Bowden refers to as the "Golden Arm"—completed 7-of-10 passes for 96 yards, and Bowden used several rushers to account for a total of 265 yards on 37 carries. Fullback Billy Hurst led the rushing attack with 94 yards on 9 carries, highlighted by his 6-yard touchdown plunge in the third quarter. While Bowden's offense chewed up the clock, his defense registered its second consecutive shutout by holding Sewanee to just six first downs.

Win No. 3
Howard 34, Tennessee Tech 0
October 3, 1959
1959 Season: 3-0

The previous season, the Bulldogs opened what would become known as Seibert Stadium. However, it took one full year before the field—which consisted for the first few seasons of only the gatehouse and east stands—would see a victory by the home team. Bowden accomplished this feat in his first home game as head coach in Birmingham, Alabama. His offense was now running at full stride as its scoring production against the Golden Eagles equaled the total points it put up in the first two games of the year. A 20-yard bullet from Milazzo to Coleman was the first score by the Bulldogs. Soon thereafter, the rout was on and Howard never looked back. Milazzo, who completed each of his first 6 passes, threw for 155 yards in the game but the other points came on the ground. Hurst, Milazzo, and running backs Ed O'Toole and Joe Hodges each scored on short bursts across the line. Howard's special teams set up Hodges's touchdown when James Reagan recovered a fumbled punt return. The Bulldogs were again outstanding on defense as

Joe Milazzo, who frequently found the end zone, was called the "Golden Arm" by Bowden.

they secured their third straight shutout and never allowed the Golden Eagle offense into the red zone.

Win No. 4
Howard 26, Millsaps 0
October 16, 1959
1959 Season: 4-1
Bowden, regrouping his team following the first loss of his coaching career, guided the Bulldogs to an easy win over the Majors—and his fourth shutout in five games. Howard started the scoring on a one-play, 2-yard run by Bobby Jackson. Jackson, in becoming the fifth different running back to score a touchdown in Bowden's first season, set up his short score with a nifty 50-yard punt return. Near the end of the first half, Millsaps drove to the Howard 2-yard line and looked to go into halftime only down a touchdown. But the Bulldog defense held tough, keeping the Majors out of the end zone on four attempts. Bowden stated that the goal-line stand was the proudest moment of his rookie season. As

13

he had done all season, Bowden reached into his bag of tricks when faced with a crucial fourth down in the third quarter. Milazzo passed to Wayne Holley. After the reception Holley pitched the ball back to Bozeman, who then scampered 20 yards for a touchdown.

Win No. 5
Howard 14, Tennessee, Martin 13
October 24, 1959
1959 Season: 5-1
This was the first game Bowden had to wait until the last second before celebrating a victory. The contest appeared as if it might turn into another rout by the visiting Bulldogs. On the opening kickoff, Versprille took a lateral and, breaking 3 tackles, sprinted the distance for a touchdown. Five minutes later the Skyhawks appeared poised to tie the game after a 6-yard touchdown on a quarterback keeper. However, the extra point was wide right, a miscue that would eventually provide the winning margin for the Bulldogs. At the beginning of the second quarter UT-Martin jumped ahead 13-7 with a 2-yard scoring run. The lead held until, with only a few minutes remaining in the game, Milazzo faked a handoff to Versprille and sprinted to the right corner of the end zone for the go-ahead score. Martin, looking for a last second victory, drove to the Howard 2-yard line before the Bulldogs stopped four consecutive runs to secure the victory.

Win No. 6
Howard 16, Southwestern 0
October 31, 1959
1959 Season: 6-1
Playing on a rain-soaked field, the Howard defenders once again stole the spotlight with their fifth shutout of the season. The Bulldogs scored first when Jackson ran over two defenders for a 20-yard touchdown. Milazzo lofted a pass to Robert Lairsey for the two-point conversion, putting Howard ahead 8-0. Jackson finished off the scoring in the third quarter when he dazzled the homecoming crowd with an impressive touchdown run. After receiving the handoff, he started to his right and looked as though he would be stopped at the line of scrimmage. Cutting to his left to avoid a defender, Jackson found daylight and outraced the defense for the 30-yard score. Bowden then turned the game over to his defense. Although Southwestern twice established time-consuming drives that moved within the Howard 10-yard line, both stalled after outstanding defensive performances. On one drive that went 75 yards and put Southwestern at the 1-yard line, Jimmy Norton came up strong and stopped a key fourth-and-goal play that preserved the shutout.

Win No. 7
Howard 24, Livingston State 0
November 6, 1959
1959 Season: 7-1
Livingston State's huge offensive line shut down Howard's running attack and the teams traded punts throughout a majority of the first half. Realizing the running game was not the

answer, Bowden turned to the passing attack and Howard began scoring easily. Milazzo threaded a beautiful pass between two defenders and Jackson raced to the 5-yard line. From the five, it took Lairsey two attempts to put the ball across the goal line and Howard was on the scoreboard. After another Lairsey touchdown, Howard put the final points on the board when Milazzo connected with Versprille for a 37-yard touchdown. Bowden, as he had done throughout the season, called for successful two-point conversions after each score. On the day, Milazzo threw for 247 yards, his highest total of the season. Milazzo mastered Bowden's Wing-T offense and ended the year with 1,282 passing yards. While Livingston State put the clamps on the Bulldogs' ground assault, Howard put up its own wall and completed its sixth shutout in Bowden's first eight games.

Win No. 8
Howard 20, Troy State 19
November 14, 1959
1959 Season: 8-1
George Versprille—who combined with Jackson and Lairsey for 1,185 rushing yards on the season—had a career game as he led the scoring and also preserved the victory with a key

Bowden watches his defense hold Livingston State scoreless.

15

fourth-quarter fumble recovery. The Bulldogs, trailing 6-0 early on, found a much-needed spark when Versprille took a punt return 77 yards for a touchdown. Howard then increased its lead soon after tackle Richard Fendley recovered a botched snap by the Red Wave. After a 24-yard pass from Milazzo to Holley moved the ball to the 4-yard line, Bowden called for two quarterback sneaks, both of which were unsuccessful. The rookie coach then asked his quarterback to try to the play a third time. The third sneak was successful as Milazzo crashed through the line for a touchdown. Troy State, trailing by one point late in the game, put together a drive that was leading to a possible winning score. The Red Wave reached the 4-yard line before Versprille recovered a fumble to preserve the one-point victory.

Win No. 9 (Textile Bowl)
Howard 52, Gordon Military 20
December 5, 1959
1959 Season: 9-1
Coach Bowden, well known for his success in postseason games, began his bowl career with a lopsided victory in this intrastate battle. Versprille followed up his all-around performance against Troy State with a three-touchdown game in the Textile Bowl—the first postseason

In preparation for the Textile Bowl, Bowden addresses his team.

contest for Howard. The Bulldogs started their rout by scoring first as Versprille went to the air. His throw found Bozeman for a 73-yard touchdown that ignited the Bulldogs and dazzled the fans attending the contest held in Fairfax, Alabama. On Howard's next possession, the Bulldogs capped a 66-yard drive with a 9-yard score by Versprille. Bowden, never afraid to call for a trick play, faced a fourth-and-long when he called for a fake punt. The play worked to perfection when Bart Kennedy hit George Raley for a touchdown. The remaining scores by the Bulldogs came on two runs by Versprille and another scamper by Lairsey. With his outstanding rookie season, Bowden not only restored life in a previously dormant football program, but he also provided a glimpse of his future leadership style and coaching acumen.

YEAR TWO: THE 1960 SEASON (8–1)

Win No. 10
Howard 14, Maryville 0
September 16, 1960
1960 Season: 1-0
For the second time in as many years, Coach Bowden's Bulldogs were facing the Scotties in the season opener. Unlike the first meeting, this game was played in severe weather because of the effects of the sixth hurricane of the year. Hurricane Ethel sent rain and wind to Seibert Stadium, which opened the door for another defensive gem by the Bulldogs. Both teams played stellar defense in the first half, with a scoreless game at intermission. But in the second half, after a long punt return by George Versprille, Howard went to a strict running game to score the first points. Versprille, Billy Hurst, and Bobby Jackson all touched the ball and quarterback Joe Milazzo scored on a 3-yard keeper and a two-point conversion run around right end to put Howard up 8-0. The Bulldogs sealed the win shortly after Johnny Shoemaker fell on a fumble. Bob Lairsey took a pitch 6 yards for the score, only four plays after the recovery. Bowden began his second season using more trickery. On three unsuspecting situations against the Scotties, he called upon his fullbacks, Hurst and Lairsey, to do quick kicks that pinned the Scotties deep in their own side of the field.

Win No. 11
Howard 56, Sewanee 0
September 23, 1960
1960 Season: 2-0
A high-scoring offense and another strong defensive outing gave Bowden a 6-0 record at home, all by shutouts. The defense, which was led by Richard Finley and Bonwell Royal, had little trouble in this sunny daytime battle against the Tennessee rival. "It was like having a barn door slammed in your face," said Tigers coach Shirley Majors, whose son, Johnny, went on to collegiate coaching success at Tennessee and Pittsburgh. Howard's offense opened it up for the Bulldogs in the second quarter with touchdown runs by Lairsey and Versprille and a touchdown pass from Shoemaker to Hurst. Bowden also provided an example of his emphasis on special teams when Julius Head, in arguably the most exciting play of the 1960 season, followed outstanding blocking to score on a 50-yard punt return.

Bowden (right) and Assistant Coach Virgil Ledbetter prepare for Sewanee.

Six different Bulldogs scored at least one of the 8 touchdowns. The win over the Tigers was the most lopsided victory in Bowden's young career.

Win No. 12
Howard 41, Georgetown 0
October 1, 1960
1960 Season: 3-0
The Bulldogs extended their season-opening shutout streak to three games—and picked up their eighth win in a row—by trouncing the Tigers. Although Bowden's boys had to travel to Kentucky for their first road game of the year, they still dominated their opponent on both sides of the ball. On defense, Jim Thompson and Carl Shepard led their colleagues in the shutout. On offense, Versprille started the rout with 2 short first-quarter touchdown runs. The running back ended the game with 99 yards on 13 carries. The defense got on the scoreboard in the second quarter when George Raley intercepted a pass and ran it back for a 27-yard touchdown. When Milazzo hit Buddy Bozeman for a 14-yard scoring strike, the first half came to an end with the game out of reach 27-0. Bowden, relying on his bench in the second half, extended his lead with touchdown runs by Hurst and Huelan Hill.

18

Win No. 13

Howard 42, Millsaps 0

October 15, 1960

1960 Season: 4-1

Facing their second Mississippi school in as many weeks, the Bulldogs came out with a vengeance against Millsaps after losing their first—and only—game of the season a week earlier in a close (24-20) contest to Mississippi College. Howard, in a night affair, again used a balanced approach to annihilate the opponent as the Bulldogs ran up 466 yards of total offense and another shutout on defense. Defensive end Don Coleman led the way in giving Bowden his ninth shutout in his first 15 games. Versprille sparked the offense in the first half with 2 early short goal line plunges. The Bulldogs went into halftime leading 20-0 after Milazzo connected with Bozeman on a 23-yard touchdown pass. After intermission, Milazzo stayed on fire and ended a drive in the third quarter with another 23-yard scoring pass to Jackson. Howard added 2 more scores on runs of 19 and 15 yards by O'Dell Ozley.

Win No. 14

Howard 28, Delta State 14

October 22, 1960

1960 Season: 5-1

Bobby Bowden has been viewed as one of the most media-friendly coaches in college football. And on this autumn afternoon, in front of 5,000 fans at Howard Stadium and thousands more via television across Alabama, Bowden made the most of his first televised contest. He pulled off the biggest upset of his young career as his underdog Bulldogs doubled up on the Statesmen from Mississippi. Milazzo passed for 2 touchdowns, one each to Raley and Jackson. Milazzo's performance was pleasing to Bowden as the coach had invited NFL great Bart Starr to camp in an effort to incorporate more of a passing attack into the Howard offense. Jackson also scored on a 23-yard run and Hurst scored on a 1-yard plunge. A tough Bulldog defense, led by defensive tackle Bennie Storie's 2 fumble recoveries, forced 3 crucial fumbles that led to scores.

Win No. 15

Howard 22, Livingston State 6

November 5, 1960

1960 Season: 6-1

The Bulldogs, while not blowing out their fellow Alabama college opponent in this night contest, used three long runs to secure the win. Howard went into halftime up 14-0 behind the strong legs of Jackson and Versprille, who combined for 204 rushing yards. Jackson, tucking the ball under his right arm, found daylight and scored the first touchdown of the game on a 52-yard run off left tackle. Versprille reached the end zone on a 50-yard scamper through a hole created by Jackson and guard Jim Thompson. The last score by the Bulldogs, the only touchdown of the second half, came on a three-play 87-yard drive capped off by Jackson's 55-yard score. Thompson again opened the hole for this long touchdown run. Linebacker Jim Norton and his defensive colleagues allowed only 171 yards of total offense.

Bobby Jackson runs through the Livingston State defense. Jackson went on to a fine coaching career in the NFL.

Win No. 16
Howard 26, Southwestern 0
November 12, 1960
1960 Season: 7-1
With only one game remaining in the season, Bowden's offense, defense, and special teams were working perfectly. The offense, led by Milazzo and Jackson, was helped out by Jackson's 70-yard touchdown on a punt return. On the play, Bowden had called for a lateral. When Head received the punt, he pitched to Jackson, who then followed a key Coleman block all the way for the score. Jackson had 115 yards rushing and a 4-yard touchdown plunge while Lairsey added a 3-yard score on the ground. The Bulldog running attack accumulated 339 yards on the ground against the Tennessee school. Milazzo directed the remaining touchdown with his 14-yard strike to Head.

George Versprille (43) was one of 15 players who transferred from South Georgia College to Howard College when Bowden became coach of the Bulldogs in 1959.

Win No. 17 (Crampton Bowl)
Howard 48, Troy State 14
November 18, 1960
1960 Season: 8-1
Six different Bulldogs made significant contributions to this state bowl win over the Red Wave in Montgomery, Alabama. Troy State relied on its quarterback Bubba Marriott for all of its offense, but his 62 passes and 2 touchdowns weren't enough to overcome Bowden's balanced game plan. The Bulldogs jumped out to a 21-0 lead in the first quarter behind touchdown runs of 31 and 8 yards by Versprille and 37 yards by Milazzo. Milazzo—who was Bowden's first Little All-American—then went to work through the air in the second quarter, hitting Bozeman for a 9-yard touchdown and James Hallman for a 46-yard scoring pass. Howard, who went into halftime with a 42-14 lead, scored one time in the second half with a touchdown pass from Shoemaker to Wayne Holley. In just two seasons as a head coach, Bowden had compiled an incredible record of 17-2.

Bowden addresses his team at halftime of the 1960 Crampton Bowl.

YEAR THREE: THE 1961 SEASON (7–2)

Win No. 18
Howard 60, Memphis Navy 0
September 23, 1961
1961 Season: 1-0
Bobby Bowden opened the season with a shutout for the third consecutive year as the Bulldogs won on the road in Memphis. On this bright and warm afternoon, both teams passed for 96 yards, but the Bulldogs' running attack and defensive schemes dominated the game. Richard Fendley, Bennie Storie, Bonwell Royal, and Carl Shepherd led Howard's defense, which forced 5 turnovers. On offense, veteran running backs Bobby Jackson and George Versprille and tailback Richard Cruce carried the load and contributed to Howard's 320 yards on the ground.

George Versprille runs through a Navy defender. In Bowden's 1961 season opener the Bulldogs totaled 320 rushing yards.

Win No. 19
Howard 64, Georgetown 6
September 30, 1961
1961 Season: 2-0
Playing their first home game of the season in the newly completed Seibert Stadium, the Bulldogs again dominated their opponent on both sides of the ball. The Tigers from Kentucky were completely overmatched as Howard ran up 459 yards on offense. The 64 points were the most scored by a Howard team since 1913. Bowden, while using almost every player on his bench, didn't use his punter because the offense never needed to punt. The only time the Bulldogs didn't convert a possession into a score was when they fumbled the ball deep in their own end zone and the Tigers recovered for their only points of the game. On the ground, Harry Hitchcock had 3 touchdowns and Bill Hurst added 2 more to lead a strong rushing attack.

Win No. 20

Howard 16, Wofford 13

October 7, 1961

1961 Season: 3-0

The Bulldogs squeaked out this victory behind two outstanding come-from-behind scores. Julius Head won the game with 55 seconds remaining when he caught a 27-yard touchdown pass from Johnny Shoemaker. Both of Howard's scores—the Head touchdown and a Buddy Bozeman fumble recovery in the end zone—came after two stellar plays by Bowden's defense and special teams. A blocked punt set up Bozeman's recovery, which put the Bulldogs up 8-7. Head's touchdown came on the very first play after the Bulldogs recovered a fumble by the Terriers.

Win No. 21

Howard 20, Delta State 14

October 21, 1961

1961 Season: 4-1

The Bulldogs were determined to please the homecoming capacity crowd of 6,000. The team also didn't want to be the first team under Bowden's leadership to lose back-to-back games. Furman had rallied around its All-American fullback Tom Campbell to beat the

With Bonwell Royal (far left) and Assistant Coach Virgil Ledbetter (third from left) looking on, Bowden (far right) awards a game ball to George Versprille (43).

Bulldogs 21-14 a week earlier. Howard had to rely on its running game and defense to pull out the win over Delta State. While the Statesmen kept within striking distance throughout this evening game, the Bulldogs led throughout the contest. Versprille capped a 61-yard first quarter drive with a 10-yard touchdown run to put the Bulldogs on the scoreboard. They added another first-quarter touchdown to go up 14-0 when Shoemaker faked the defense with a perfectly executed 65-yard bootleg run. For the second consecutive win, Howard's final score of the game came on a fumble recovery. The Bulldog defense, led by Carl Shepherd's 24 tackles, held the Statesmen to solo scores in the second and fourth quarters.

Win No. 22
Howard 18, Carson-Newman 7
October 28, 1961
1961 Season: 5-1
Bobby Jackson made the most of his 10 carries as he had 206 yards on the ground against the Eagles. The star running back put the Bulldogs ahead in the first half with a touchdown run and added 2 more scores in the second half. One of his second-half scores came on an 80-yard run while a double reverse set up the other. Although Bowden's strategy failed to result in a touchdown, it did produce a 70-yard gallop by Jackson that set up his short plunge into the end zone.

Win No. 23
Howard 34, Southwestern 7
November 11, 1961
1961 Season: 6-2
For the second time this season, the Bulldogs had to rebound after a loss. The previous week, Bowden went for broke—and lost—against Mississippi College. After Head scored on an 85-yard kickoff return to bring the Bulldogs to within one point (15-14), Bowden called for a two-point conversion. When it failed, Howard lost to the Choctaws for the third straight season. And for the first time in Bowden's career, he had lost more than one game in a season. Against Southwestern, Head—once again—stole the spotlight with touchdown receptions of 37 and 27 yards from Shoemaker. The game against the Lynx, while featuring additional touchdowns from the regulars such as Hitchcock, Jackson, and Versprille, also provided an opportunity for outstanding performances by two previously unheralded players, tight end Charles Jacobs and fullback Terrell Humphreys.

Win No. 24
Howard 80, Troy State 0
November 18, 1961
1961 Season: 7-2
Coach Bowden has never had a more one-sided victory than this 80-0 triumph. The 80 points resembled a score in basketball, a sport Bowden coached for one year in 1955 at South Georgia College. Bowden, in addition to his role as athletics director and football coach at South Georgia College, also ran the baseball program for three years. From the

coin toss, the Red Wave didn't stand a chance. On the first play from scrimmage, Jackson took a handoff and ran 80 yards for a touchdown. Howard found the end zone 8 times on the ground, 3 times through the air, and 1 time on a punt return. This blowout was the second-highest scoring game in the history of football at Howard, and the most points for the Bulldogs since an 87-0 win in 1907. Shepherd, Storie, and tackles James Hallman and Jerry Pharo led Howard's stellar defensive performance.

YEAR FOUR: THE 1962 SEASON (7–2)

Win No. 25
Howard 22, Chattanooga 13
September 15, 1962
1962 Season: 1-0
The Bulldogs were undermanned to start the season, as quarterback Johnny Shoemaker, tackle Richard Fendley, and halfback Jerry Busby were held out of the season opener due to preseason injuries. Howard got on the board at the end of a 58-yard drive when running back Bobby Jackson scored on an 11-yard run. Early in the second half, Buddy Bozeman read a screen perfectly and picked off a Chattanooga pass, returning it 51 yards for the score. Reggie Allen scored Howard's final touchdown on a 17-yard romp through the middle of

Reggie Allen cuts back for a touchdown.

the defense. Bowden went for two and was successful when Garland Jones caught the conversion in the corner of the end zone.

Win No. 26
Howard 40, University of Mexico 0
September 29, 1962
1962 Season: 2-0
Playing before a statewide television audience and a home crowd of over 4,500 fans, the Bulldogs had no trouble with the Pumas. Howard scored early in the first quarter when Bozeman took a pitch from Ray Collins and weaved his way for a 36-yard touchdown. Larry Hitchcock added another score near the end of the first half when he crashed through the line for a 1-yard touchdown run. Jackson all but secured the win when he recovered a Puma fumble on the 15. Three plays later, Jerry Partridge strolled into the end zone for another touchdown. Late in the third quarter, Ed Donahoo broke through several attempted tackles for a long 72-yard gain. Richard Cruce then finished the drive—and the game's scoring— with a 9-yard touchdown run.

Win No. 27
Howard 14, Louisiana College 12
October 6, 1962
1962 Season: 3-0
An impressive goal-line stand on a two-point conversion followed by a blocked field goal attempt secured the win for the Bulldogs. Although Bowden's squad jumped to a two-touchdown lead by halftime, Howard still needed spectacular plays late in the game from unlikely heroes to preserve the win. Jackson started the scoring on a 12-yard run that capped an impressive 68-yard drive. With time running out in the first half, Bozeman leaped to make a great catch in the end zone to give Howard a 14-0 lead. Louisiana College then scored 2 unanswered touchdowns and lined up for a two-point conversion to tie the game. But Bozeman and Harry Hitchcock drilled the rusher and prevented the extra points. Louisiana College again moved the ball easily to the 35 and with 12 seconds remaining called time out to allow the kicking game to get ready for the winning field goal. Wayne Howard eluded a defender and blocked the kick, ending the low-scoring affair.

Win No. 28
Howard 14, Furman 7
October 13, 1962
1962 Season: 4-0
Bowden faced one of his toughest foes when his Bulldogs went on the road to meet Furman, a stronger team from the Southern Conference. Furman had no plans on losing as Howard was slated as the homecoming opponent. But the Bulldogs broke into the scoring column early in the second quarter when Bill Hurst faked right and leaped left over the Furman defense for a 7-0 lead. The Howard lead did not last long, as Furman scored on the very next possession. The Bulldogs responded and, facing a third-and-long near the end of the third quarter, Bozeman made an incredible diving catch to keep the drive alive. Seven plays

Bill Hurst jumps over the goal line.

later, Harry Hitchcock bullied his way into the end zone, carrying several defenders with him. Bowden's friends, while congratulating him on the major victory against a more powerful team, also have teased him because of one peculiar call. Bowden, without a kicker who could convert anything longer than an extra point, punted from Furman's 19 rather than attempt a field goal. Of all his wins at Howard, Bowden considers this huge upset his favorite.

Win No. 29
Howard 47, Carson-Newman 0
October 27, 1962
1962 Season: 5-1
After losing for the first time this season when they played Delta State the week before, the Bulldogs looked to regroup and get another winning streak started. They did just that as Bowden picked up his 15th shutout in only 33 career games. Several Howard players provided key plays in the blowout. Bozeman, who had his 100th career reception in the game, caught 2 touchdown passes. Larry Wyatt intercepted two passes, returning one 65

yards for a touchdown. The loss to the Statesmen the game before was costly, as the Bulldogs lost Jackson to an injury. But against the Eagles, Cruce filled in wonderfully, running for 89 yards and a touchdown.

Win No. 30
Howard 21, Mississippi College 3
November 3, 1962
1962 Season: 6-1
Throughout his career, Bowden has had only a couple of teams that were consistently difficult for him to defeat. Mississippi College was his first such opponent, losing to them his first three times. His final game against this school, however, was different thanks to Reggie Allen. Although it looked early like Allen would be the goat, he quickly regained the confidence of his coach and led the Bulldogs to victory. On Howard's second play of the game, Allen fumbled and Mississippi College capitalized with a field goal for an early lead. Bowden kept his faith in Allen, who rebounded to have a career game. First, he returned a punt for a 45-yard touchdown early in the second quarter. Then, in the third quarter, Allen scored on a reverse that covered 23 yards. He finalized the scoring with a 2-yard plunge near the end of the fourth quarter.

Buddy Bozeman (80) blocks as Reggie Allen (43) heads up field.

Win No. 31
Howard 34, Wofford 28
November 10, 1962
1962 Season: 7-1

The match-up between these two teams featured wide-open offenses on a colder than normal day in November. The Bulldogs, as they did most of the season, quickly gained an early lead. Allen continued his hot streak as he scored on a 5-yard run and a 15-yard pass. With the score 14-6 and five seconds remaining in the first half, Shoemaker lofted a short Hail Mary into the end zone. The prayer was answered when Cruce hauled it in for a touchdown and a 20-6 halftime lead. Wofford started the second half with a touchdown and the teams alternated scoring until the final gun. The 34-28 victory would be Bowden's last as the head coach at Howard. The Bulldogs would lose three weeks later to McNeese State in the Golden Isles Bowl. Bowden would complete his tenure at Howard with a record of 31-6. With six children at home, Bobby and Ann decided it was time to move on to higher-paying positions. In 1963, they moved to Tallahassee, where Bowden became an assistant coach under Bill Peterson at Florida State University. Bowden was in charge of coaching the wide receivers. Among his talented players was T.K. Wetherell, who became president of FSU in 2003. After working as an assistant coach at Florida State starting in 1963 and then at West Virginia starting in 1965, Bowden accepted the head coaching position at WVU in 1970.

Bowden completed his career at Howard College with a record of 31-6, including 15 shutouts.

PART II
BOWDEN JOINS THE BIG TIME
WEST VIRGINIA UNIVERSITY (1970–1975)
WINS 32–73

YEAR FIVE: THE 1970 SEASON (8–3)

Win No. 32
West Virginia 43, William & Mary 7
September 12, 1970
1970 Season: 1-0
Bobby Bowden came to West Virginia University (WVU) for an opportunity to build a perennial winner and pick up an annual salary of $25,000. When he took over at WVU, he told Mountaineer fans to expect a high-scoring, crowd-pleasing offense and a strong defense. Bowden did not wait long to make good on his promise. In game one, his new team rolled up 623 yards of offense while holding Lou Holtz's Indians to three first downs in the first half and only 1 touchdown for the game. Running back Pete Wood led the offense with 167 yards, including touchdown runs of 21 and 35 yards. Quarterback Mike Sherwood scampered for a touchdown and threw for 2 other scores. Despite being far from his roots and his coaching mentor, Bowden continued to pattern his game after Bear Bryant. He kept

West Virginia's Mountaineer Field as it looked in 1970 when Bowden arrived.

as updated as possible on Bryant's career, including subscribing to Birmingham newspapers throughout his tenure at WVU.

Win No. 33
West Virginia 49, Richmond 10
September 19, 1970
1970 Season: 2-0
Although the final score would indicate otherwise, Bowden's Mountaineers received a huge scare before breaking the game open in the second half. Trailing 10-7 with the first half coming to an end, Leon Jenkins sparked West Virginia. Jenkins received a punt on the 37 and used a Dave Morris block to reach the end zone. Wood scored rushing and receiving touchdowns early in the second half to put the game out of reach. Sherwood, who completed 9-of-10 passes, directed the offense, which set the school record with 640 total yards and tied another mark with 30 first downs.

Bowden discusses Dale Farley's injury with reporters after the Virginia Military game.

Win No. 34

West Virginia 47, Virginia Military 10

September 26, 1970

1970 Season: 3-0

In this warm-weather meeting, the Mountaineers scored early and often to handily defeat the Keydets. After a short kickoff return, West Virginia scored quickly on two long plays. Wood took the opening snap 36 yards with a tough run. On the second play, Bob Gresham looked to be stopped near the line of scrimmage before reversing his direction and sprinting 43 yards for the score. With the offense scoring at will, the defense held VMI to only 137 total yards. In what Bowden would later call the toughest break of the season, middle linebacker Dale Farley injured his knee and would miss several games.

Win No. 35

West Virginia 16, Indiana 10

October 3, 1970

1970 Season: 4-0

The Mountaineers traveled to Indiana looking for their first win in 48 years against a Big Ten opponent. Although West Virginia came into the game averaging 46 points a contest, a gusty wind seriously handicapped both offenses. Tight end Jim Braxton single-handedly won the game for WVU with his pass receiving and kicking. Braxton scored the Mountaineers' only points of the first half with a 23-yard field goal. With touchdowns in each of the third and fourth quarters, along with the final extra point, Braxton accounted for every point scored by West Virginia.

Win No. 36

West Virginia 24, Colorado State 21

October 24, 1970

1970 Season: 5-2

For the first time in his career, Bowden had to rally his troops after back-to-back losses. Bowden still refers to the second setback—a 36-35 shocker against Pittsburgh in the "Backyard Brawl" after the Mountaineers led 35-8 at halftime—as one of his worst coaching memories. Against the Rams, WVU jumped out to a quick lead. Ahead 21-7 early in the contest, the Mountaineers held on at the end for the win. Touchdowns by Sherwood, Eddie Williams, and Frank Samsa made the game look like a rout. Bill Samuelson's fourth-quarter kick proved to be the difference as the Rams mounted a comeback—including a 97-yard kickoff return for a touchdown.

Win No. 37

West Virginia 28, East Carolina 14

November 7, 1970

1970 Season: 6-3

After a loss to Penn State one week earlier, the Mountaineers went on the road looking to start another winning streak. Sherwood was brilliant, throwing for four touchdowns including a 65-yard strike to Braxton. Averaging 28 yards on his 5 receptions, Braxton scored twice in the game. The Pirates attempted to move the ball with their strong running attack but could manage only 168 yards on the stingy WVU defense.

Win No. 38
West Virginia 28, Syracuse 19
November 14, 1970
1970 Season: 7-3
Once again, the Mountaineers jumped out to a commanding lead only to hang on for the victory. Beautiful passes from Sherwood to Wayne Porter accounted for 45- and 27-yard touchdowns. Sherwood's quarterback sneak staked WVU to a 21-0 lead through the third quarter. Syracuse then scored on three consecutive drives, bringing the score to 21-19. With under six minutes remaining, Syracuse looked to go ahead with first-and-goal from the 2-yard line. Farley, seeing significant action for the first time since his injury seven weeks earlier, stopped the run on first down. Danny Wilfong stopped a second-down run. Farley and Danny Smith combined to stop Syracuse again setting up fourth and goal. Wilfong, Smith, and Farley became heroes as they ended the scoring threat with a stop at the one. Syracuse would get the ball again but Farley intercepted a pass to close out the victory.

Leon Jenkins
returns a punt.

Bowden shouts instructions to Bernie Galiffa during the first game of the 1971 season.

Win No. 39

West Virginia 20, Maryland 10

November 28, 1970

1970 Season: 8-3

Bowden has used his quarterbacks effectively to establish a tremendous coaching record in Atlantic Coast Conference (ACC) games. His knack for using his signal callers against ACC opponents began with this game as he picked up his first career victory over a team in his future conference. Sherwood directed the offense as he threw touchdown passes to Braxton and Chris Potts. Samuelson added short and mid-range field goals and two extra points to account for the rest of the Mountaineer scoring. Bowden's defense played a crucial role in the victory, intercepting 3 passes to end long drives. Gresham, who ended the game as the school's career rushing leader, ran for 165 yards. With an eight-win season, Bowden had restored credibility to the WVU program and enthusiasm to Mountaineer fans.

YEAR SIX: THE 1971 SEASON (7–4)

Win No. 40

West Virginia 45, Boston College 14

September 11, 1971

1971 Season: 1-0

As anticipation for Bowden's second year grew, media and fans labeled the upcoming season "Excitement '71." The first game lived up to that billing, as West Virginia's offense scored easily, capitalizing on 5 fumble recoveries and 3 interceptions. Running back Pete Wood scored 2 touchdowns and ran for a school-record 214 yards, an amazing feat considering the wet, slippery conditions. Quarterback Bernie Galiffa also ran for 1 touchdown and passed to Harry "the Snake" Blake for another. The defensive highlight came when linebacker Wib Newton snatched up a fumble and struggled 11 yards through several Eagles for a touchdown.

Win No. 41
West Virginia 16, Richmond 3
September 25, 1971
1971 Season: 2-1
After losing to California the previous week, Bowden looked to rebound in his only night game of the season. The defense was stellar, limiting the Spiders to only 176 total yards. Flanker Chris Potts started the scoring with a 16-yard reception from Galiffa. Shortly after halftime, Frank Nester booted a 31-yard field goal to give West Virginia a 9-3 lead. The final score came when Wood took a Galiffa pitch to the right and leaped over the defense for a 3-yard touchdown, giving Bowden his 10th win at WVU.

Win No. 42
West Virginia 20, Pittsburgh 9
October 2, 1971
1971 Season: 3-1
Bowden learned about the intensity of the West Virginia and Pittsburgh rivalry in his rookie campaign when the Mountaineers built a huge lead only to lose in the final seconds. In this season's contest, after an early field goal by Pitt, Kerry Marbury scored 2 touchdowns with a Panther touchdown sandwiched between them to make the score 13-9 at the half. A fourth-quarter quarterback sneak by Galiffa accounted for the final victory margin. "Buckley's Bandits"—the name given to the defensive backfield coached by Hayden Buckley—had four interceptions that stopped several scoring threats by the Panthers.

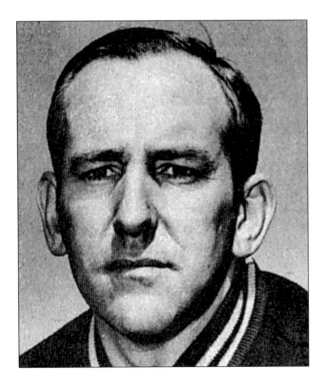

WVU Assistant Coach Hayden Buckley was the leader of "Buckley's Bandits."

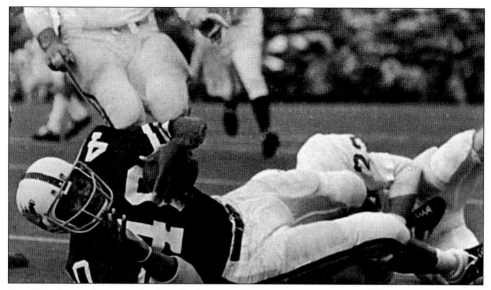

Pete Wood scored twice in back-to-back games.

Win No. 43

West Virginia 28, William & Mary 23

October 9, 1971

1971 Season: 4-1

Two future legendary coaches and friends met for the second time when Bowden's Mountaineers faced Lou Holtz's Indians. Although WVU scored easily on its first possession with a touchdown run by Wood, the game was not decided until the final two minutes. After the early score, the Indians scored 3 unanswered touchdowns to take a commanding lead. But an incredible 65-yard punt return by Leon Jenkins gave the Mountaineers a big lift and set up a short Kerry Marbury score. After trading punts, West Virginia took the ball and capped off a 63-yard drive with a 4-yard touchdown by Wood. Then, with only 2:22 remaining in the game, Bowden created magic when he called for a long bomb that worked to perfection. Galiffa hit Nate Stephens in stride for the 64 yard winning touchdown.

Win No. 44

West Virginia 44, East Carolina 21

October 16, 1971

1971 Season: 5-1

Bowden used a swarming defense and seven sophomore starters to pull out this relatively easy win. The Pirates committed four turnovers, each leading to Mountaineer scores. Two early touchdowns by Wood and a field goal by Nester gave the Mountaineers a 16-0 second-quarter lead. Bowden's team then coasted, scoring 14 points in each of the final two quarters. The highlight was one of Wood's scoring runs when he weaved left, right, and left again before eventually finding the end zone for a 35-yard touchdown.

Both Kerry Marbury (22) and Pete Wood were injured against Temple.

Win No. 45

West Virginia 43, Temple 33

October 23, 1971

1971 Season: 6-1

A come-from-behind victory, a record-breaking rushing performance, and two key injuries made for an intense battle between the Mountaineers and Owls. Trailing 33-29 with just under five minutes remaining and WVU on its own 18-yard line, Bowden reached again for the long bomb. Galiffa launched a missile to Blake, who hauled it in and, with his incredible speed, outran the defenders for a 50-yard touchdown. A local writer would later call this the "pass of the decade." The win was costly, especially with Penn State on deck. Marbury, who left the game in the second half with a leg injury, set the West Virginia single-game rushing record against the Owls with his 291-yard performance. His backfield teammate, Wood, was also injured in the game.

Win No. 46

West Virginia 28, Virginia Military 3

November 13, 1971

1971 Season: 7-3

Injuries dashed a season of anticipation and led to back-to-back losses to Penn State and

Duke. One injury that was particularly devastating occurred when Newton was knocked out for the season with a knee injury. The injuries and losses also ate away at West Virginia's confidence, resulting in 5 interceptions against the Blue Devils. Against the Keydets, Bowden was forced to go to a simplified offensive attack. Keeping the ball on the ground for most of the game, the Mountaineers ate the clock with scoring drives of 80, 72, and 64 yards. Galiffa ran for 2 short scores while Wood added another. The last WVU touchdown was set up by a 62-yard David Morris interception return. On the day, the Mountaineers rushed for 301 yards and passed for only 71, somewhat atypical for Bowden-coached teams. While misfortune kept Bowden out of postseason play for the second consecutive year, the following season Bernie Galiffa and Danny Buggs made sure their coach received a bowl invitation.

YEAR SEVEN: THE 1972 SEASON (8–4)

Win No. 47
West Virginia 25, Villanova 6
September 9, 1972
1972 Season: 1-0
Bobby Bowden entered his third season with the Mountaineers returning 17 starters. While the experienced starters led the way throughout the season, it was kicker Frank Nester, who led West Virginia to its season-opening victory. Nester tied an NCAA record with 6 field

Bowden's daughter Robyn (top row, third from left) was the WVU head cheerleader in 1972.

goals as the Mountaineers scored 25 unanswered points after the Wildcats got on the board first. Kerry Marbury rushed for 95 yards and the Mountaineers only touchdown while Bernie Galiffa passed for 195 yards. The defense, led by David Morris, had four interceptions to the delight of Robyn Bowden. The coach's daughter headed the Mountaineer cheerleading team and later married defensive back Jack Hines, who went on to a coaching career with Auburn and Clemson. With his daughter on the sideline and future son-in-law on the field, the season was truly a family affair.

Win No. 48
West Virginia 28, Richmond 7
September 16, 1972
1972 Season: 2-0
The Mountaineers used a pro-type, wide open passing attack on offense featuring the "Veer" and "I" formations. Bowden attempted to take advantage of his quick skill players by using a formation that included two running backs, two wide receivers, and a tight end. He liked his outside speed and quickness so much that he referred to his talented receivers as the best group in the nation. WVU won its second straight home game as Bowden took advantage of the quick artificial surface to jump out to a big lead on the Spiders. Comfortably ahead most of the game, Bowden elected to keep the ball on the ground, where Marbury rushed for 175 yards. The Mountaineer receivers—most notably budding sophomore superstar Danny "the Rabbit" Buggs—provided the highlights.

Win No. 49
West Virginia 48, Virginia 10
September 23, 1972
1972 Season: 3-0
Galiffa threw four touchdown passes to earn national quarterback-of-the-week honors. But it was the threat of Buggs that led to Bowden's first road win of the season. Early in the second quarter, Galiffa threw the ball long and high, letting Buggs run underneath it for a 78-yard score. On the next possession, Buggs—whom Bowden referred to as "Lightning Bug"—again outraced the defender, this time from 23 yards. Bowden, knowing the Cavaliers were fearful of his wide receiver's speed, called for a fake reverse to Buggs that had all defenders chasing the run as Galiffa easily threw to a wide-open Marshall Mills for a touchdown.

Win No. 50
West Virginia 49, William & Mary 34
October 7, 1972
Season: 4-1
The game was not as close as the final score indicates, as Buggs made sure that the Mountaineers would not lose two weeks in a row. After falling on the road to Stanford, Bowden turned Buggs loose against the Tribe. Buggs was everywhere, catching 6 passes for 140 yards, returning punts for 28 yards, and using Bowden's favorite play—the reverse—to account for 100 yards rushing. The Morgantown crowd was in awe as Buggs took a reverse

Bernie Galiffa starred at quarterback throughout the 1972 season.

late in the game and cut against the grain three times while eluding six defenders for a 37-yard touchdown. John "Tree" Adams and Tom Zakowski each recovered fumbles that led to easy WVU scores.

Win No. 51
West Virginia 31, Tulane 19
October 21, 1972
1972 Season: 5-2
After the second road loss of the season, Bowden was happy to return home even if it meant facing a much-improved Tulane squad. Early in the game, Ron Lee scored twice as the two teams fought for a lead. Zakowski set up both Lee scores with an interception and fumble recovery. On the day, the Mountaineers intercepted 5 Green Wave passes. One pickoff by Doug Charley led to a Marbury touchdown before Buggs sealed the win. Although Bowden did not count on his superstar to carry the entire load, Buggs once again provided a spectacular highlight. Fielding a punt on the five, Buggs leaped over one defender, broke a tackle, stiff-armed through two opponents, and pulled away from seven others chasing him for a 95-yard touchdown, a feat Bowden called "amazing."

Kerry Marbury scored on a 55-yard run to start the game against Pittsburgh.

Win No. 52
West Virginia 38, Pittsburgh 20
November 4, 1972
1972 Season: 6-3
A loss to Joe Paterno's Penn State team seven days earlier meant Bowden had alternated wins and losses for six straight games. With the physical Panthers, Bowden knew his team would have to control the ball to pull out the road win. Marbury started the contest with a 55-yard score on the first possession. After a defensive stop, Galiffa hit Nate Stephens and the lead was 14-0. Despite a comeback by Pitt to tie the game, Bowden made sure his team did not panic. After a Nester field goal and another Marbury score, WVU led 24-14 at halftime. In the second half, Bowden's offense controlled the ball with time-consuming drives and his defense stopped the Panthers three times inside the West Virginia 20 to preserve the win.

Win No. 53
West Virginia 50, Virginia Military Institute 24
November 11, 1972
1972 Season: 7-3
While the game saw several Mountaineer team records fall, an injury to Marbury late in the contest limited Bowden's offense attack for the remainder of the season. Buggs once again made his case for All-American status as he scored on a punt return, reception, and yet another reverse. WVU put up its highest point total of the season and tied the highest point

total of Bowden's career at West Virginia. Galiffa's 194 yards passing enabled him to become the first Mountaineer to throw for over 2,000 yards in one season. While the team broke a total of seven records on the day, Bowden was most proud of breaking the team record for most touchdowns (50) and interceptions (22) in a season. "You can't win without scoring and you can't score without the ball," Bowden told reporters, as he reflected on the records.

Win No. 54
West Virginia 43, Syracuse 12
November 18, 1972
1972 Season: 8-3
With Marbury out and a bowl invitation on the line, Bowden turned to Buggs to earn the right to play in the postseason. Buggs started his day with a 77-yard touchdown reception on a pass from Galiffa. On the next possession, with all eyes looking for the reverse, Bowden called for the fake reverse to Buggs and the Orangemen fell for it. Galiffa had plenty of time to connect with Stephens for 61 yards and six points. After three defensive stops, Buggs took a handoff 33 yards for his second score and ended his day with a reverse of 80 yards that Syracuse Coach Ben Schwartzwalder called the best run of the season. The victory earned Bowden's troops a birth in the Peach Bowl, where they were defeated 49-13 by Lou Holtz and North Carolina State.

Danny Buggs was spectacular
against Syracuse.

YEAR EIGHT: THE 1973 SEASON (6–5)

Win No. 55
West Virginia 20, Maryland 13
September 15, 1973
1973 Season: 1-0
Around Morgantown, pre-season All-American wide receiver Danny Buggs was known as "Dangerous Dan." The junior proved to be just that in the season opener at College Park when, with the score tied at 13 and only 32 seconds remaining, he received a punt at the Mountaineer 31-yard line. When he found no daylight to his left, he reversed his position and ran backwards until he spotted an opening that led all the way to the end zone with only eight seconds remaining. West Virginia, while leading 6-0 at halftime, trailed by a touchdown with five minutes remaining. Quarterback Ade Dillon looked off two receivers before finding running back Dwayne Woods for a 75-yard touchdown to tie the game. Buggs then performed his spectacular punt return. While the offense and special teams received most of the credit for the win, the WVU defense recovered 2 fumbles, intercepted 2 passes, and allowed the Terps only 175 yards of total offense.

Win No. 56
West Virginia 24, Virginia Tech 10
September 22, 1973
1973 Season: 2-0
Bowden's Mountaineers needed only one quarter to put away the Hokies—and give

*Arthur Owens eludes a
defender for a long gain.*

Bowden his 25th win at WVU—in the season's home opener. In front of over 33,000 fans, the Mountaineers fell behind 3-0 in the second quarter only to come back over the next 13 minutes with 24 unanswered points to go into halftime up 24-3. While Dillon threw another long (59 yards) touchdown to Buggs and Woods and Arthur Owens each scored short rushing touchdowns, the story of the game was a spectacular goal-line stand by the West Virginia defense. After pass interference gave the Hokies a first-and-goal at the 2-yard line, the Mountaineers stuffed all four running plays behind the strength of Jeff Merrow, John Adams, Tom Zakowski, and Charlie Miller.

Win No. 57
West Virginia 17, Illinois 10
September 29, 1973
1973 Season: 3-0
According to Bowden, this was his biggest win before arriving at Florida State. Illinois, at home and coming into the game undefeated, appeared to be an unbeatable opponent for the Mountaineers. Two consistent themes, however, changed that for West Virginia. Bowden's defense was superior for the third consecutive game and his wide receiver, Buggs, was again outstanding. Buggs caught a 55-yard touchdown from Dillon for the winning score with only 3:25 remaining in the game. The defense, led by Merrow's 18 tackles and Zakowski's 17 tackles, allowed only a first quarter touchdown and a second quarter field goal to the highly touted Fighting Illini. WVU's other two scores came on a 13-yard run by fullback Mike Nelson in the second quarter and a third-quarter field goal by Frank Nester.

Danny Buggs (8) was spectacular against Illinois but missed the Indiana game due to an injury.

45

Win No. 58
West Virginia 20, Miami 14
November 2, 1973
1973 Season: 4-4

West Virginia, after building a 3-0 record, endured a tough October. The Mountaineers went winless in the month with losses to Indiana, Pitt, Richmond, and Penn State. The loss to Indiana, coached by Lee Corso, was understandable because Buggs sat out the game with a thigh injury. "Beating West Virginia without Danny Buggs," commented Corso, "is not really beating West Virginia." In the loss to Pitt, Bowden lost Dillon for the season to a separated shoulder. Richmond intercepted 6 West Virginia passes as the Spiders took advantage of the inexperience of Dillon's replacement, Chuck Fiorante. Sophomore Ben Williams, the third string quarterback in September, was the starter against Penn State. In the loss, Williams showed potential as he found Buggs for a 96-yard score—the longest touchdown pass in school history. By the time the Mountaineers made the trip to the Orange Bowl to face Miami, WVU was playing for pride, as any postseason hopes had been eliminated. Down 14-13, Williams led the Mountaineers on a 95-yard drive capped off when he hit Marshall Mills for a 32-yard touchdown to give the Mountaineers the win. The quarterback's all-around game was highlighted by a 4-yard bootleg run and a 12-yard connection with Buggs for another score.

Win No. 59
West Virginia 42, Virginia 17
November 17, 1973
1973 Season: 5-5

After a 25-13 loss to Boston College the week before, the Mountaineers evened their record in the home finale against the Cavaliers. With quarterback injuries and inexperience, Bowden adjusted his strategy to a ground attack. The change worked to perfection as WVU ran for 388 yards while passing only 8 times for 42 yards. Woods, who led the Mountaineers in rushing in 1973 but sat out the 1974 season with a knee injury, had 178 yards rushing and 3 touchdowns while Arthur Owens ran for 136 yards and 2 touchdowns. Williams added another rushing score as West Virginia put up a season-high total on the scoreboard.

Win No. 60
West Virginia 24, Syracuse 14
November 24, 1973
1973 Season: 6-5

Bowden came into the game facing the possibility of his first losing season as a head coach. But a dominating defensive performance kept Bowden's winning streak alive as the Mountaineers recovered four first-quarter fumbles and had 5 recoveries in the game. Rain, which started to fall right before the opening kickoff, continued throughout the game and eventually turned the Syracuse field into a muddy pit. West Virginia never looked back after scoring first in the opening quarter on Williams's 9-yard option run. In the second quarter, Williams put the Mountaineers up for good on a 13-yard touchdown pass to co-captain Dave Jagdmann. A 56-yard touchdown return by defensive back Marcus Mauney

Bowden explains his point in the wet conditions.

with just over a minute remaining preserved the win and the winning season. In a year that started out with great promise after the victory over Illinois, injuries dashed all postseason hopes. Still, Bowden managed to end the season on a two-game winning streak to improve his winning percentage at WVU to .644, the highest of any head coach since Clarence Spears in the early 1920s.

YEAR NINE: THE 1974 SEASON (4–7)

Win No. 61
West Virginia 16, Kentucky 3
September 21, 1974
1974 Season: 1-1
The media predicted Bowden's team would open the season 1-1, but they did not anticipate the way it happened. After suffering an upset loss at home to Richmond in the season opener, West Virginia bounced back, beating a strong Kentucky team in Morgantown. The Mountaineers began with an impressive 99-yard drive, capped when Heywood Smith burst over the goal line. Emil Ros booted a 24-yard field goal and Ron Lee found the end zone in the second quarter to end the WVU scoring. Bowden's defense held Sonny Collins, the

The 1974 WVU media guide featured Bowden and All-American Danny Buggs.

much-publicized Wildcat running back, to only 57 yards on 12 carries. Arthur Owens proved to be the best back in the game carrying for 100 yards on 7 carries.

Win No. 62
West Virginia 24, Indiana 0
October 5, 1974
1974 Season: 2-2
After a close loss at Tulane, the Mountaineers recovered to record the only shutout for Bowden during his career at WVU. Against the Hoosiers, Bowden decided to give Chuck Fiorante the start against a tough Indiana team. Fiorante showed his skills in the second quarter, leading the Mountaineers to 21 points. Ben Williams ran for a 2-yard score to start the scoring and Lee scampered from 8 yards for another. Fiorante then lofted a 9-yard pass into the corner of the end zone that Marshall Mills hauled in for the third touchdown. Ros drilled all three extra points, along with a 39-yard field goal late in the third quarter to end the scoring. The Mountaineers used a basic 5-2 defensive formation throughout the season. It proved particularly effective against the Hoosiers. Ray Marshall provided 3 tackles-for-losses and Ken Culbertson and Bruce Huffman each recorded 12 stops to lead West Virginia's impressive defensive performance.

Win No. 63
West Virginia 39, Syracuse 11
November 9, 1974
1974 Season: 3-6
For the second consecutive year the Mountaineers went on a four-game losing streak. After losses to Pittsburgh, Miami, Penn State, and Boston College, Bowden pulled off his third consecutive victory over Syracuse. West Virginia scored early with touchdown runs of 46 and 9 yards by Owens, who ended the year with 1,130 yards rushing. All-American Danny Buggs showed why he earned that honor when he hauled in a 62-yard Kirk Lewis pass to put Bowden's team ahead 20-0. With the outcome no longer in doubt, Bowden sent in heralded freshman Dan Kendra (whose son would later play for Bowden at Florida State) for his first collegiate experience. Kendra wasted no time showing the coach his talent, hitting Marshall Mills for a 33-yard touchdown with his first college pass. Kirk Lewis added a late fourth-quarter score to end the scoring for WVU.

Win No. 64
West Virginia 22, Virginia Tech 21
November 23, 1974
1974 Season: 4-7
At first glance it would appear that a season finale between teams with losing records would hold little excitement. But, wanting to end the season on a positive note, the Mountaineers

Arthur Owens scores from the 9-yard line.

played one of the best games of the season in a game marked with special plays. Marcus Mauney put the Mountaineers on the board first when he picked off a Virginia Tech pass and ran it back 99 yards for the most electrifying play of the year. After the Hokies scored with just over six minutes remaining to give them a 21-14 lead, Kendra led the Mountaineers on a six-play, 63-yard drive with Bernie Kirchner scoring from the 10 to put WVU within one point. Not wanting to settle for a tie, Bowden elected to go for a two-point conversion. Kendra then hit Mills with a beautiful pass and the Mountaineers finished the season with a victory. While the season ended on a winning note, the earlier mid-season swoon gave Bowden his first losing season—one of only two he would endure throughout his entire career. The low point of that first losing season came in the loss to Pitt, after which he was hung in effigy around campus. Another time, Bowden discovered that someone had placed a "For Sale" sign in his front lawn. Despite the backlash, Bowden decided to stay on board after the school president, athletics director, athletics committee, and trustees rallied to his support.

Bowden discusses the 1974 season with reporters.

YEAR TEN: THE 1975 SEASON (9–3)

Win No. 65
West Virginia 50, Temple 7
September 13, 1975
1975 Season: 1-0
Bobby Bowden was coming off his toughest year of coaching. Although he was tempted to leave after that season, he stayed for another year and turned the program around. Against the visiting Owls, the Mountaineers jumped out to a 14-0 halftime score behind rushing touchdowns by Dwayne Woods and Arthur Owens. West Virginia then scored 5 touchdowns in the second half, beginning with a 47-yard touchdown run by Owens, who ended the game with 127 yards. Other second-half scores came on a 1-yard run by Danny Williams and a 4-yard touchdown pass from Dan Kendra to tight end Bubba Coker. Two touchdowns were scored on interception returns as Chuck Braswell ran his back 63 yards in the third quarter and Tom Pridemore returned his pickoff 87 yards for the game's final score.

Win No. 66
West Virginia 28, California 10
September 20, 1975
1975 Season: 2-0
Eighteen lettermen returned on offense for Bowden's final season at West Virginia. One of the deepest positions was the offensive backfield with three seniors (Owens, Ron Lee, and Heywood Smith) and one junior (Woods). At Berkeley, it was Smith who had a career day, as the fullback ran for 146 yards and 2 touchdowns. This was the first and only time Smith went over the century mark in his career. Bowden relied on his running game to produce the other scores with Lee's 1-yard rush and Owens's 4-yard scamper. The defense, led by linebackers Steve Dunlap and Ray Marshall, held California's All-America running back Chuck Muncie to 107 yards on the ground.

Win No. 67
West Virginia 35, Boston College 18
September 27, 1975
1975 Season: 3-0
Bowden handed over the quarterback position to Dan Kendra, a 6-foot-1, 200-pound sophomore, who had thrown for 316 yards and 3 touchdowns in 1974. Bowden relied on his ground game throughout most of the 1975 season, but it was Kendra's second-half quarterback sneak for a touchdown and his 150 passing yards that helped WVU pull out the win over the visiting Eagles. Lee had 3 short rushing touchdowns while Woods added 102 yards on 7 carries.

Win No. 68
West Virginia 28, Southern Methodist 22
October 4, 1975
1975 Season: 4-0
The Mountaineers had an experienced and talented offensive line. Tackles Dave Van Halanger and Tom Brandner, guards Steve Earley and Bob Kaminski, and center Al Gluchoski opened impressive holes for West Virginia's running backs. Van Halanger would go on to become a longtime strength and conditioning coach for Bowden's Seminoles. Against SMU in the Cotton Bowl, the line cleared the way for the Mountaineers to rush for 408 yards. Owens had 171 yards while Woods added another 103 yards and 3 touchdowns in the close win in Dallas. After the victory over the Mustangs, the Mountaineers lost back-to-back games as they turned the ball over at Penn State and allowed a strong comeback by visiting Tulane.

Win No. 69
West Virginia 10, Virginia Tech 7
October 25, 1975
1975 Season: 5-2
West Virginia celebrated the 50th anniversary of Mountaineer Field in 1975. Bill McKenzie celebrated his first career field goal in a close win at home against the Gobblers. With the score tied 7-7 at the beginning of the third quarter, defensive back Chuck Braswell forced a fumble that defensive end Gary Lombard recovered. McKenzie then entered and booted his game winner. In the game, Owens rushed for 102 yards to break Bob Gresham's school record of 2,181 career-rushing yards.

Win No. 70
West Virginia 38, Kent State 13
November 1, 1975
1975 Season: 6-2
Bowden searched all season to find replacements for departed wide receivers Danny Buggs, Marshall Mills, and Bernie Kirchner. Although Bowden had his son (and future coaching opponent) Tommy at wide receiver, the junior had only a limited impact. As Bowden noted before the season, "Tom lacks the range of past receivers but he'll lay it on the line." In week eight, Bowden saw the emergence of three pass catchers as Scott MacDonald, Bubba Coker, and Randy Swinson all caught touchdown passes. Kendra threw 2 touchdowns while Danny Williams threw the third against the Golden Flashes. Two school records were established in the win as Owens ran for 171 yards and McKenzie hit his 28th straight extra point.

Win No. 71
West Virginia 17, Pittsburgh 14
November 8, 1975
1975 Season: 7-2
With Florida State representatives in the stands to observe Bowden's performance, the legendary coach pulled off one of his favorite wins in dramatic fashion over the rival

Tommy Bowden was a wide receiver for his father at West Virginia University. He would later coach against his dad in the first football contest between father and son as coaches.

Panthers. As Bowden would later tell Steve Ellis of the *Tallahassee Democrat*, "That win got me the Florida State job." In the game, with the scored tied at 14-14, Kendra threw a 26-yard strike to Swinson, who hustled out of bounds with four seconds remaining. McKenzie then hit a 38-yard field goal as time expired and WVU had one of its biggest wins in the 68 meetings between the two schools. While many saw the game on ABC television, those in attendance swarmed from the stands and rushed Mountaineer Field to celebrate the win. The game was an evenly matched contest as the two schools came in with the same record and very similar rushing attacks. West Virginia was able to get on the board first in the third quarter when Ray Marshall recovered a Tony Dorsett fumble that set up Lee's 1-yard touchdown run. Owens then added a 23-yard rushing touchdown in the fourth quarter.

Win No. 72
West Virginia 31, Richmond 13
November 15, 1975
1975 Season: 8-2
Strong defensive performances by Steve Dunlap and Tom Pridemore allowed the visiting Mountaineers to take a 24-0 halftime lead and cruise to an easy win over the Spiders. West Virginia's first score came when Dunlap intercepted a pass in the first quarter that set up a 1-yard touchdown run by Lee. After McKenzie kicked a field goal, Pridemore recovered a fumble in the second quarter that set up 5-yard touchdown run by Smith. Later in the quarter, Pridemore intercepted a pass that led to Smith's second score, a 17-yard run. Danny Williams added a 1-yard rushing touchdown in the fourth quarter to end the scoring.

Win No. 73 (Peach Bowl)
West Virginia 13, North Carolina State 10
December 31, 1975
1975 Season: 9-3

Coach Bowden left West Virginia a winner. Not only did he lead the Mountaineers to an outstanding regular season, he also guided them in a bowl win in a revenge game against the Wolfpack. Bowden's Mountaineers had lost to North Carolina State in the Peach Bowl three years earlier. In 1975, it appeared the Wolfpack would earn another win in Atlanta as they went ahead 10-0 in the second quarter. But Kendra hit Owens for a 39-yard touchdown on the last play of the first half and West Virginia went into halftime down 10-6. The Mountaineers took their lead in the fourth quarter when Kendra, who was named the outstanding offensive player, threw his second touchdown. Scott MacDonald caught Kendra's pass and raced 50 yards for the winning score. The West Virginia defense held the Wolfpack scoreless in the second half thanks to the leadership of Ray Marshall, who was named the game's outstanding defensive player. After the bowl win, Bowden escaped the snow and fickle fans of West Virginia for the vacant position in Tallahassee. He knew that Florida State provided him an opportunity to work on building a dynasty. Not lost in the decision was the fact that he also knew he could work on his other favorite activity—golf—year round. In addition to his deep interest in history, traveling, military battles, and boxing, Bowden is a golf fanatic. The combination of potential with FSU football and pleasure on the golf course proved irresistible. So, Bobby loaded up the moving truck and departed WVU with a 42-26 record and a 73-32 career mark.

Bowden, with wife, Ann, look over the Doak Campbell stadium after his arrival at FSU.

PART III

THE GAMBLER TAKES A CHANCE

FLORIDA STATE UNIVERSITY (1976–1986)

WINS 74–163

YEAR ELEVEN: THE 1976 SEASON (5–6)

Win No. 74
Florida State 20, Kansas State 10
October 2, 1976
1976 Season: 1-3

Before Bobby Bowden decided to come on board, Florida State was such a losing program with a small stadium and even less tradition that there was talk about dismantling the program. The Seminoles were $600,000 in the red and, as noted by Bowden, "couldn't get much lower" than the 4-29 mark they had established over the three years before his arrival. Doak Campbell Stadium "was a skeleton" when he arrived in Tallahassee. "It resembled more of an erector set than a stadium." The Seminoles had little recruiting or publicity. "When I got here, the Gators had telecasts throughout the state. For FSU, there was

Doak Campbell Stadium (1976) witnessed few victories before the arrival of Bowden but expanded 10 times after his first year.

nothing on the air before I got here." But the coach, who was never afraid to take a chance with his play calling, took a gamble with his move to the rolling hills of Tallahassee. FSU president Stanley Marshall and athletics director John Bridgers convinced Bowden to move back "home" and become the school's eighth head coach. The $37,500 base salary offer—an increase of $12,500 over his salary at WVU—helped make the decision a little easier for Bowden. It took a little patience before the risk finally began paying off. Before his first year at Florida State, Bowden had recorded only one losing season in his 10 years as a head coach. He knew coming in that his expectations were much higher than many of his FSU fans. "When I was at Alabama, all I heard was 'Beat Auburn.' When I was at West Virginia, all I heard was 'Beat Pitt.' When I got to FSU, their bumper sticker read, 'Beat Anybody.'" Although he went 5-6 in his inaugural season, it was the one and only losing record throughout his illustrious FSU career. After the third game, however, Florida State officials were beginning to question their decision to bring in Bowden. In a 21-12 loss at Memphis State, the Seminoles had four turnovers. Florida State again committed costly turnovers at Miami, which resulted in a 47-0 thrashing. The Seminoles took an early lead at Oklahoma, only to watch the Sooners score on a fumble recovery that led to a 24-9 setback. After the three opening road losses, the Seminoles were glad to be in Tallahassee for the home opener against the Wildcats in front of a crowd of 30,353. Florida State fell behind early 10-0 before scoring 20 unanswered points in the second half. Quarterback Jimmy Black, who traded signal calling duties with Clyde Walker, found Ed Beckman in the end zone for a 17-yard score in the third quarter and hit Kurt Unglaub on a 26-yard pass for the final touchdown of the game. Dave Cappelen hit two extra points and 2 field goals in the win.

Win No. 75
Florida State 28, Boston College 9
October 9, 1976
1976 Season: 2-3
The Seminoles traveled to Boston for their fourth road trip in five games. FSU went on top for good when senior running back Rudy Thomas finished a drive with a 12-yard scoring run late in the first half. Florida State came out hot in the second half with Black finishing the opening drive of the quarter with a 10-yard quarterback keeper. Mark Lyles and Rudy Maloy completed the scoring with touchdowns (1-yard touchdown run and 65-yard fumble return for a touchdown, respectively) in the fourth quarter. Although the Eagles came into the contest with a perfect 3-0 record, they were unable to secure another win in large part to four fumbles. Three of those miscues led to scores by the Seminoles.

Win No. 76
Florida State 30, Southern Mississippi 27
November 6, 1976
1976 Season: 3-6
In a season of streaks, the Seminoles again lost three consecutive battles to formidable foes (Florida, Auburn, and Clemson). Florida State got back on the winning track with their home game against the Golden Eagles. Southern Mississippi had a 27-10 lead after three quarters of play. Then, in one of the most explosive quarters and dramatic comebacks of

Bowden poses with 1976 team captains Rudy Thomas (33), Jimmy Black (16), Joe Camps (42), and Jeff Leggett (30).

Bowden's career, the Seminoles scored 20 unanswered points over a 7:23 span in the fourth quarter for the 3-point win. All 3 scores (10-yard run, 4-yard run, and a 95-yard touchdown reception) in the fourth quarter were by Thomas. The 95-yard pitch and catch from Black to Thomas set a school record, which lasted a mere two weeks.

Win No. 77
Florida State 21, North Texas State 20
November 13, 1976
1976 Season: 4-6
The field was covered with 4 inches of snow after a Texas winter blizzard had swept through Denton. Despite 6 FSU turnovers, Jeff Leggett scored a 7-yard touchdown with just over two minutes remaining to bring the Seminoles within one point of a tie. Bowden, as had become his custom when he had the option to go for the tie or win, decided to use a trick play to go for the win. With 2:13 left on the clock, running back Larry Key hit wide receiver Kurt Unglaub for a two-point conversion to put the Seminoles ahead 21-20 and give Florida State its second two-game winning streak of the season.

Win No. 78
Florida State 28, Virginia Tech 21
November 20, 1976
1976 Season: 5-6
For the third consecutive game, Bowden engineered a comeback win after trailing in the

fourth quarter. This time, Bowden relied on a freshman quarterback to come off the bench and save the day. Jimmy Jordan, who had been the backup to Black all season, entered the game in the fourth quarter and led the Seminoles down the field on both of his drives. The first drive, which ended with a 33-yard touchdown pass to Jackie Flowers, tied the game. Jordan's second offensive possession, a much quicker drive, ended with a school-record, 96-yard scoring pass to Unglaub, giving FSU the winning touchdown. In the win over the Hokies, Bowden began to establish himself as a big-play coach by engineering long and spectacular touchdowns. Key, who became Florida State's career rushing leader, had a school-record 97-yard touchdown run in the first quarter. Black hit wide receiver Mike Barnes for a 75-yard score in the second quarter. Bowden, while not providing a winning season in his first year at Florida State, did give Seminole Nation a glimpse into what the next three decades would hold for them on the football field. In a season of streaks, the Seminoles ended the year with three consecutive wins and the strong foundation for the upcoming season.

YEAR TWELVE: THE 1977 SEASON (10–2)

Win No. 79
Florida State 35, Southern Mississippi 6
September 10, 1977
1977 Season: 1-0
Little did people know that this game against the Golden Eagles would be the birth of two legends in Tallahassee: Bowden's dynasty of years without a losing season and the arrival of freshman noseguard Ron Simmons. By the time his career was over, Simmons was the second-leading tackler in Florida State history with 483 tackles. As Bowden told *Athlon Sports* decades later, "It's hard to say one man can make or break your program, but look what Tony Dorsett did for Pitt. We feel the same way about Ron Simmons." Although Simmons's college career ended in 1980, Bowden's winning streak would continue for over a quarter-century. Coach Bowden relied on Simmons and defensive end Scott Warren to begin his second year on a positive note. FSU's special teams gave the Seminoles their first points when Warren scored on a short return following a blocked punt by Simmons. The offense, which had looked impressive during fall drills, finally came together over the final two quarters behind the two-headed attack of Jimmy Jordan and Wally Woodham. The quarterbacking combo, both of whom graduated from Leon High School in Tallahassee and were elected into the FSU Athletic Hall of Fame in 1985, led a 28-point second half explosion and connected with 10 different receivers for 265 yards.

Win No. 80
Florida State 18, Kansas State 10
September 17, 1977
1977 Season: 2-0
Although the visiting Seminoles trailed in the second and fourth quarters, they bounced back each time and used a 10-point effort in the final seven minutes to pull out the win.

Jordan sealed the win by hitting Mike Shumann on a 36-yard touchdown pass with 2:17 remaining. Larry Key led the ground game with 120 yards. Supporting the balanced offensive attack was—for the second consecutive week—an outstanding defensive performance. Bowden's defense allowed 78 passing yards and only 2.1 yards a carry on 48 rushing attempts. Kansas State's 2 scores came on a 50-yard blocked punt return and a short field goal, set up by an interception that placed the Wildcats in scoring position. The victory was Bowden's fifth consecutive win, dating back to the final three wins of the 1976 season.

Win No. 81
Florida State 25, Oklahoma State 17
October 1, 1977
1977 Season: 3-1
Following a close (23-17) home loss to Miami, the Seminoles traveled to Stillwater. The Cowboys were the Big Eight Conference co-champions in 1976 and were expecting a similar run behind 1977 Heisman Trophy candidate Terry Miller. But the Seminoles—after trailing 17-3—rallied around their seasoned running back to pull out their second consecutive fourth-quarter comeback on the road. Key established a school record—broken 21 years later by Travis Minor—by carrying the ball 32 times. Key's workload contributed to his season total of 239 carries, a record that still stands at Florida State. In addition to his seventh 100-yard rushing game of his career (127 yards), Key added 72 yards on 3 receptions and 60 yards on a kickoff return. On the strength and speed of Key's legs, the Seminoles scored 22 unanswered points over the final two quarters. Florida State eventually took the lead (18-17) with 6:46 remaining on Dave Cappelen's 30-yard field goal. The last score—a 19-yard touchdown connection between Woodham and Key—gave the Seminoles an eight-point victory.

Win No. 82
Florida State 14, Cincinnati 0
October 8, 1977
1977 Season: 4-1
On this early October evening in Tallahassee, Bowden once again made the right decision by calling on Woodham to work his magic on the field. His quarterback choice hit Shumann with a 15-yard touchdown pass at the end of the second quarter for the first score of the game. Early in the third quarter, Woodham found Roger Overby for a 36-yard score. The 2 touchdown passes were more than enough as the defensive unit held its opponent scoreless for the first time since 1974. The shutout was both particularly impressive (as the Bearcats came in undefeated) and fairly ironic (as it was the Cincinnati defense that was ranked nationally in five categories). Woodham ended the game 16-of-23 for 265 yards. Nine of his completions were to Overby, who had a career game with 136 yards. Overby's breakthrough performance was pleasing to Bowden as the receiver—only seven months earlier during spring practice—had considered giving up his pursuit of football.

Win No. 83

Florida State 24, Auburn 3

October 22, 1977

1977 Season: 5-1

Several streaks were broken and records established during this rout of the Tigers. In 10 previous meetings with Auburn, Florida State had never secured a win. Bowden, however, had no trouble defeating the Tigers in his first meeting on a warm, fall evening at Doak Campbell Stadium. Furthermore, the victory was the first for the Seminoles over a Southeastern Conference opponent since 1972. On offense, Key again led the ground game, establishing a single-game rushing record (170 yards) with 2 touchdowns on 25 carries. Florida State defenders, who entered the game holding opponents to 11 points per game, sustained their outstanding performance. Ron Simmons, Aaron Carter, and linebacker Jimmy Heggins held the Tigers' scoring production to only a second-quarter field goal. Simmons, a 1986 FSU Athletic Hall of Fame inductee, had a fumble recovery and 19 tackles (10 solo) while Carter added 5 tackles and Heggins had 4.

Win No. 84

Florida State 35, North Texas State 14

October 29, 1977

1977 Season: 6-1

Ron Simmons, whose brilliant play on defense Bowden compared to Tony Dorsett's offensive efforts at the University of Pittsburgh two years earlier, continued to add to his tremendous freshman season. A homecoming crowd of nearly 41,000 cheered on the new Tallahassee hero as he had 5 sacks and—for the second consecutive week—19 tackles, His sack performance, which is still an FSU record, earned him numerous honors including the AP Lineman of the Week and *Sport Illustrated*'s Defensive Player of the Week. The Florida State defenders rallied around their teammate and even scored twice in the first half. The first score came when Bobby Butler blocked a punt that was returned for a 15-yard score by Ivory Joe Hunter to give the Seminoles a 14-7 lead in the second quarter. Only 44 seconds later, Willie Jones recovered a fumble in the end zone to give the home team a 21-7 lead at halftime. The offense added 2 touchdowns in each of the final two quarters with 1-yard runs by Woodham and Key.

Win No. 85

Florida State 23, Virginia Tech 21

November 5, 1977

1977 Season: 7-1

Throughout his career, Bowden had the ability to coach out a win against the Hokies. Bowden's 14 career wins without a loss against Virginia Tech are the second most victories he has against any opponent. He has the most victories (16) against none other than the archrival Florida Gators. Against the Hokies, Bowden's Seminoles traveled to Blacksburg as homecoming opponents. Bowden relied on strategy and a high-octane offense to overcome the rain and a fourth-quarter deficit. From the sideline he called four reverses. Shumann, who gained 99 yards on the first three reverses, ran the fourth reverse as well.

However, instead of keeping the ball, Shumann—who also led Florida State with 80 receiving yards—hit Overby for a 39-yard completion. The play set up Cappelen's game-winning 29-yard field goal with just under five minutes remaining. The Seminoles racked up 442 yards on offense while holding the Hokies to 14 passing yards.

Win No. 86
Florida State 30, Memphis State 9
November 13, 1977
1977 Season: 8-1
The Tigers entered Doak Campbell with a strong running game. While the Memphis State rushers ran often (53 carries), Bowden's defenders had little trouble slowing down the ground attack, holding the Tigers to 60 yards. The Florida State defense also set up the first touchdown. After a fumble recovery by Heggins, Woodham hit Shumann for a 27-yard touchdown near the end of the second quarter to give Florida State a 10-0 lead at halftime. The Seminoles scored 20 consecutive points in the second half to soundly defeat the Tigers. A 13-yard touchdown pass from Jordan to Greg Lazzaro capped off Florida State's scoring streak. The win over the Tigers in front of just over 40,000 fans was the sixth in a row for the Seminoles. The winning streak ended the following week when Florida State traveled to California and was thumped 41-16 by San Diego State.

Win No. 87
Florida State 37, Florida 9
December 3, 1977
1977 Season: 9-2
With impressive wins over Oklahoma State and Auburn, the Seminoles had already established 1977 as one of the best years in Florida State history. However, Bowden needed to defeat Florida in order to bring his program national recognition and overcome an impenetrable roadblock. The Seminoles, who had the unenviable task of traveling to Gainesville and facing its largest crowd (63,563) of the season, had lost nine consecutive games to the Gators. Florida State established itself as the better team early in the contest by holding Florida on its first drive and then moving the ball 72 yards on a drive that was capped by a 35-yard touchdown pass from Woodham to Unglaub. Jordan, who took over in the second quarter, threw 3 touchdowns to earn offensive player of the game honors from ABC. Woodham and Jordan combined for 326 passing yards. Overby was the preferred target for both Jordan and Woodham as he had 6 receptions for 124 yards and 3 touchdowns. Shumann, playing in his final regular season game, caught 5 passes for 111 yards. On the ground, Larry Key became the first Florida State running back to rush for 1,000 yards in a season when he ran for 143 yards against the Gators. While the offense received most of the attention, the Florida State defense was outstanding, holding Florida to 3 field goals and 200 yards of total offense. For the first time in four regular seasons the Gators were kept out of the end zone. Bowden still ranks this win as one of the best in his career. In only his second year with the Seminoles, he had now given Florida State its first ever nine-win regular season. More importantly, as he had hoped, he had turned the program around by routing the rival Gators.

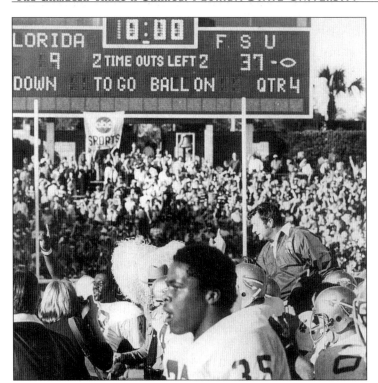

Bowden is carried off the field after defeating Florida.

Win No. 88 (Tangerine Bowl)
Florida State 40, Texas Tech 17
December 23, 1977
1977 Season: 10-2

In the 29 years before Bowden's arrival at Florida State, the Seminoles had been to just eight bowls. For the first time in seven years, the Seminoles were invited to a bowl and traveled to Orlando to face the Red Raiders. Florida State never trailed and dominated the game over the final three quarters. Key's 93-yard kickoff return in the second quarter opened up the contest and the Seminoles never looked back. Jordan, coming off his spectacular performance against Florida three weeks earlier, had his best game and took home the offensive MVP trophy. He completed 18-of-25 passes for 311 yards and 2 touchdowns. His first score, a 37-yard pass to Grady King, gave Florida State a 16-3 halftime lead. His second touchdown throw was a 40-yard bomb to Shumann in the third quarter. Woodham added 2 touchdown passes over the final two quarters. Key completed his outstanding Florida State career with one of his best all-around performances. The record-breaking crowd of 44,502 witnessed his performance as he rushed 21 times for 83 yards, caught 6 passes for 100 yards, and had 3 kick returns for 131 yards. Willie Jones, a player Bowden considers one of the best defensive ends he ever coached, was named defensive MVP. With the win, Florida State became the first school from the State of Florida to post a 10-win season.

Scott Warren (80), who started all but one game during Bowden's first four years at Florida State, went on to a medical career and was inducted into the FSU Athletics Hall of Fame in 1997.

YEAR THIRTEEN: THE 1978 SEASON (8–3)

Win No. 89
Florida State 28, Syracuse 0
September 9, 1978
1978 Season: 1-0
Seminole Nation had high expectations for the season after Bowden doubled Florida State's season win total in his second year. Playing on a warm Syracuse afternoon, FSU scored the only touchdown of the first half when Jimmy Jordan crashed through two Orangemen defenders for a 1-yard touchdown run. With no scoring in the third quarter, FSU went on a 98-yard drive early in the final stanza. Facing a third and nine from the three and just looking to give the punter room, Jordan hit his high-school teammate, Kurt Unglaub, for a 37-yard gain and the drive continued. Jordan completed the drive by hitting Grady King with a 4-yard touchdown pass. Later in the same quarter, Wally Woodham replaced Jordan at quarterback and found Jackie Flowers for a 15-yard score to put Florida State ahead 21-0. The game was finally secured after Gator Cherry rumbled 9 yards for the final score. Although he did not figure in the scoring, Holmes Johnson accounted for 135 of the team's 304 rushing yards.

Win No. 90
Florida State 38, Oklahoma State 20
September 16, 1978
1978 Season: 2-0
Playing their first home game of the season, the Seminoles looked like they would go into halftime behind 6-3. However, in a span of 19 seconds, they went ahead 17-6 at the break.

Chief Osceola and Renegade, college football's top tradition, took the field for the first time before the 1978 Oklahoma State game.

With 1:40 remaining in the half, Mike Kincaid recovered a Cowboy fumble. Jordan capitalized on the turnover when he hit Johnson with a 35-yard pass on the very first play after the change of possession. The Cowboys fumbled on their next possession and Willie Jones pounced on the loose ball, giving the Noles one more chance to score before the half. Again, on the very first play, Jordan threw a touchdown pass. This time it was a 32-yard strike to Unglaub. Two more touchdowns from Johnson and a 1-yard run by Mark Lyles ended the Seminole scoring.

Win No. 91
Florida State 31, Miami 21
September 23, 1978
1978 Season: 3-0
Bowden's teams have often relied on a strong defense stepping up for the big games. Against the Hurricanes, the Seminoles intercepted Miami quarterbacks—including starter Mark Richt (who would later become an assistant under Bowden)—3 times, recovered 2 fumbles, and blocked 1 punt. With the defense on the field and trailing 7-0, Ron Simmons blocked a punt, which Mark Macek returned 42 yards to tie the score. After another Miami touchdown and just before halftime, Florida State scored on a 4-yard pass from Jordan to Flowers. Woodham, who replaced Jordan early in the second half, scored from the 1-yard line to put FSU ahead 21-14. Dave Cappelen added a 26-yard

field goal to go ahead 24-14. After Richt closed the gap to 24-21 and the Miami defense stopped FSU on three plays, the Seminoles punted and again relied on their defense to hold on. Bobby Butler intercepted the next Miami pass and returned the ball 40 yards. The interception set up a 22-yard touchdown pass from Woodham to Lyles and secured the victory.

Win No. 92

Florida State 26, Cincinnati 21
October 7, 1978
1978 Season: 4-1
The Seminoles needed a miracle finish against the Bearcats in order to return to their winning ways after a stinging 27-21 loss to Houston a week earlier. In the third quarter, Cincinnati appeared poised to pull off the upset when the visitors went ahead 21-14 on a short touchdown run. Then midway through the fourth quarter Florida State mounted an impressive drive and ultimately scored on a 5-yard pass from Jordan to King. Not interested in a tie, Bowden elected to go for the win with a two-point conversion. However, Woodham's pass fell incomplete. The Seminole defense kept any hope alive as they stopped Cincinnati on the next series. After three unproductive offensive plays, the Seminoles faced a fourth-and-22 from their own 46-yard line and under two minutes remaining on the clock. On fourth down, Jordan threw a perfect pass and hit Sam Platt in stride, resulting in a 54-yard, game-winning touchdown.

Win No. 93

Florida State 38, Southern Mississippi 16
October 28, 1978
1978 Season: 5-3
Bowden decided to juggle his lineup after back-to-back losses to Mississippi State and Pittsburgh. The loss to the Panthers was particularly hard for him to take as his offense managed only three points. Against the Golden Eagles, Woodham joined the starting lineup for the second time this season. Greg Ramsey opened the scoring with a 2-yard run and Cappelen added a 30-yard field goal to give the Seminoles 10 quick points. The two teams traded scores and the Seminoles led 17-14 as they headed to the locker room. Woodham threw 3 of his 4 touchdown passes in the second half. He hit Flowers with touchdown passes of 23 and 61 yards to put the game out of reach. Near the end of the contest, Woodham connected with King for a 14-yard touchdown. Woodham finished with 237 yards on 16-of-24 passing.

Win No. 94

Florida State 24, Virginia Tech 14
November 11, 1978
1978 Season: 6-3
Bowden effectively used a balanced offense to secure a come-from-behind victory over the Hokies. On the ground, Johnson gained 152 yards (the most of any Seminole during the 1978 season) and scored a touchdown. Through the air, Woodham connected with eight

different receivers. Trailing 14-10 at the half, Bowden's defense shut out Virginia Tech the rest of the game. The Florida State defense held the Hokies to only 76 passing yards and 139 rushing yards.

Win No. 95
Florida State 38, Navy 6
November 18, 1978
1978 Season: 7-3
Bowden is a legend for having his teams well prepared for the biggest games. The 1978 homecoming game against the nationally ranked Midshipmen was no exception. Playing before the then second-largest home crowd in stadium history (45,795) and an ABC audience, the Seminoles dominated the entire game. Leading 10-6 early in the third quarter, Bowden turned it into a throw-and-catch exhibition by Jordan and Platt. Jordan completed touchdown passes to Platt on three straight possessions, including a 51-yard strike for the third score. Simmons led the defense with 7 solo tackles (including 3 for a loss), 3 assists, and a fumble recovery.

Win No. 96
Florida State 38, Florida 21
November 25, 1978
1978 Season: 8-3
In what was becoming commonplace at Doak Campbell, a record crowd (48,432) witnessed Florida State's second consecutive victory over the Gators. With 2 short touchdown runs

Kurt Unglaub was a big-play receiver from 1976 to 1979.

by Lyles and a 40-yard Woodham-to-Platt bullet for another score, FSU was ahead 21-0 in the first 13 minutes. Florida responded with 3 unanswered scores of their own and the teams went into halftime 21-21. Bowden knew the Seminoles were in an advantageous position even though the score was tied. His defense had not allowed a second half point in the last five games. This game would make it six straight as the defense kept Florida from scoring another point. After trading punts to begin the second half, Florida State marched 71 yards on 13 plays to take the lead. An impressive 7-yard run by Johnson accounted for the scoring. The Seminoles extended the lead with a Cappelen 29-yard field goal and a Woodham 1-yard touchdown leap (set up by Scott Warren's interception and ensuing return to the Florida 3-yard line).

YEAR FOURTEEN: THE 1979 SEASON (11–1)

Win No. 97
Florida State 17, Southern Mississippi 14
September 8, 1979
1979 Season: 1-0
The anticipation of the summer was fulfilled during the 1979 campaign when the Seminoles went undefeated during the regular season, Bowden was honored as the National Coach of the Year, and the "Voice of the Seminoles" (Gene Deckerhoff) began his radio broadcasting of FSU games. "I enjoy my relationship with Gene more than any other professional relationship," Bowden once said. "Everyone loves Gene." The first win came in the season opener, a game when Bowden is nearly unbeatable. In fact, during his 27 seasons at Florida State's helm, he has only lost three times to begin a season. The 1979 opening game produced a victory, but the outcome was in doubt until Florida State rallied to score 2 touchdowns in the final 10 minutes. A 26-yard Dave Cappelen field goal was the only score FSU could manage in the first three quarters. Trailing 14-3 in the fourth quarter and needing a big break, Monk Bonasorte laid out to block a Southern Mississippi punt that the Seminoles recovered on the 15-yard line. Jimmy Jordan then hit Jackie Flowers with a perfect pass for a touchdown, making the score 14-9 as the two point attempt was unsuccessful. Bowden's defense then forced the Golden Eagles to punt. Gary Henry, who had called 6 fair catches throughout the day, knew the team needed another spark and fielded the punt with several defenders nearby. Henry darted back-and-fourth across the field and ended with a 65-yard touchdown return for Bowden's eighth fourth-quarter comeback at Florida State.

Win No. 98
Florida State 31, Arizona State 3
September 15, 1979
1979 Season: 2-0
The Seminoles and Sun Devils arrived at Tampa Stadium poised for a shootout as both teams were nationally ranked offensive powers. A dominating defense and 9 fumbles led to the FSU rout. Bonasorte again made the big plays, picking off a pass that led to the only score of the first quarter—an 18-yard pass from Wally Woodham to Flowers. Bonasorte,

who would end the season leading the nation with 8 interceptions, later intercepted his second pass of the game, and on the next offensive play Greg Ramsey broke free for a gain of 50 yards down to the 1-yard line to set up the second score. On the very next Sun Devil possession, FSU forced a fumble that Ron Simmons recovered on the Arizona State 8-yard line. Florida State capitalized on the turnover, scoring quickly on a pass from Jordan to Grady King. In the fourth quarter, Jordan directed a 10-play, 86-yard drive that chewed up most of the clock and ended with his 15-yard touchdown pass to Jimmy Williams to complete the scoring—giving Bowden his 25th win at FSU.

Win No. 99
Florida State 40, Miami 23
September 22, 1979
1979 Season: 3-0
Bowden's two-quarterback system of Woodham and Jordan had been praised for its tremendous passing ability. But, against the Hurricanes, Bowden used the running attack to account for 205 yards and defeated first-year coach Howard Schnellenberger. The win over Miami was Florida State's first in six attempts and first ever at Doak Campbell. The always-reliable Cappelen put Bowden's group on the board early with a 26-yard kick. Miami countered with a touchdown, and then Florida State scored the next 30 points. Following a touchdown by Mark Lyles, Butler intercepted a Miami pass, leading to another Cappelen field goal. Short touchdown runs by Lyles and Ramsey—behind the blocking of Gil Wesley, Mike Good, Ken Lanier, Greg Futch, and Tom Brandon—and a 57-yard punt return for a touchdown by Henry put the game out of reach.

Bowden and his interchangeable quarterbacks, Wally Woodham (12) and Jimmy Jordan (15) pose for the cameras during media day.

Win No. 100
Florida State 17, Virginia Tech 10
September 29, 1979
1979 Season: 4-0
Against the undefeated Hokies, the game was broadcast by ABC—meaning it was time again for the region to see one of the best defenders ever to put on an FSU jersey. Simmons collected his third ABC player of the game award after making 8 tackles, including 3 for a loss. Trailing 7-0 late in the first quarter, Ramsey broke 2 tackles and ran 16-yards for a touchdown. As the second quarter came to a close, Bowden elected to control the clock. The decision resulted in a 14-play, 80-yard drive that ended when Jordan hit Flowers with a perfect 18-yard pass for the score. The second half was dominated by the defense, with each team only managing a field goal. Bowden's offense totaled 436 yards, including 183 passing yards by Woodham and 139 by Jordan.

Win No. 101
Florida State 27, Louisville 0
October 6, 1979
1979 Season: 5-0
The shutout at Louisville stretched Bowden's winning streak to nine consecutive games. In his 326 games at the helm of FSU, Bowden shut out the opponent 20 times. Special teams and a strong defense—led by Simmons, Scott Warren, Arthur Scott, Jeremy Mindlin, and Mark Macek—won the game for the Seminoles. Two safeties by the FSU defense and a blocked punt by Ed Richardson that was recovered by Butler for a touchdown accounted for 11 Seminole points. Bowden's defenders put up their best performance of the year as

Ron Simmons, who went on to an outstanding professional wrestling career, was arguably the greatest Seminole defender of all time.

they held the Cardinals to 7 yards rushing. Louisville did not fare much better in the air, gaining 86 yards passing against linebackers Reggie Herring and Paul Piurowski and defensive backs Keith Jones, Ivory Joe Hunter, Butler, and Bonasorte. Florida State again showed a versatile offense with 2 scoring passes from Woodham and 118 rushing yards from Lyles.

Win No. 102

Florida State 17, Mississippi State 6

October 13, 1979

1979 Season: 6-0

With a scoreless tie early in the second quarter in front of a record-setting crowd (48,701) at Doak Campbell, Florida State got on the board first with a 1-yard touchdown burst by Mike Whiting. After the Bulldogs punted, Jordan finished off a drive when Flowers out-fought a defender to haul in a 17-yard touchdown pass. Cappelen finished the FSU scoring with a 46-yard field goal late in the third quarter. With just over a minute remaining, the Bulldogs avoided a shutout with a 2-yard touchdown run. The six points were the first allowed by the Florida State defense—ranked fourth in the nation—in over eight quarters.

Win No. 103

Florida State 24, Louisiana State 19

October 27, 1979

1979 Season: 7-0

This win is another Bowden favorite, both for the victory on the field and the decision he made surrounding it. Bowden, who before the game billed it as the biggest game in Florida State history, had a major decision to make as his team traveled to Baton Rouge for this nationally televised game. Louisiana State—looking for a coach who could beat Alabama's Bear Bryant—was trying everything to lure Bowden away from FSU. The lobbying was very effective. In fact, Bowden had told his wife, Ann, that he would probably accept the offer if his Seminoles lost at Tiger Stadium. In the game, Bowden abandoned his platoon quarterbacking system and went with Jordan the entire game. Woodham had opened the previous 10 games, but Jordan was brilliant against the Tigers as he passed for 312 yards and 3 touchdowns. After Bonasorte recovered a Louisiana State fumble on the second play of the game, Jordan connected with Platt for a 3-yard score. The Tigers responded by scoring 2 touchdowns before Jordan took control. Another LSU fumble led to a Jordan bomb to Hardis Johnson for a 53-yard touchdown. After a scoreless third quarter, Flowers caught a 40-yard touchdown pass from Jordan after the ball had glanced off an LSU player. "We're now for real," said Flowers, who ended the game with 6 catches for 174 yards. After the win, Bowden stated he, "realized that maybe we could get it done right here at FSU. And I've never regretted it." Within two weeks of the game, he signed a long-term contract with the Seminoles for an annual salary of $128,000. On November 5th, the day he agreed to the deal, he announced that he wanted "to be the head coach at Florida State from now on because we're going to build tradition into this program." He then added, "hopefully, this thing is going to last forever."

Win No. 104

Florida State 26, Cincinnati 21

November 3, 1979

1979 Season: 8-0

For the second straight year, Bowden found his team heavily favored but trailing Cincinnati by double digits in the second half. Behind 21-7 late in the third quarter, Woodham connected with Lyles for an 8-yard touchdown to make the score 21-13 after a failed two-point conversion. On their next possession, the Seminoles conducted a 10-play drive that ended when Woodham hit Flowers for a 5-yard touchdown. After an injured Simmons returned to the game and helped force the Bearcats to punt on their next possession, the Seminoles drove to the 9-yard line, where they lined up for a game-winning field goal. But, instead of a kick, Woodham handed off to Whiting, who raced through the defense for the win.

Wally Woodham led FSU to a victory over Cincinnati.

Win No. 105

Florida State 27, South Carolina 7

November 10, 1979

1979 Season: 9-0

In a battle between the sixth-ranked Seminoles and the No. 19 Gamecocks, Cappelen outshined South Carolina All-American George Rogers. Cappelen, who would end his career with a then school-record 240 points, kicked four field goals to single-handedly outscore the Gamecocks. The Florida State defense held South Carolina to 51 passing yards and only nine first downs. "We got whipped real good," South Carolina coach Jim Carlen admitted after the game. "Bobby has done a heck of a job here." The win moved Bowden ahead of his friend Don Veller into third place in FSU coaching victories with 32 wins. Yet another record-breaking crowd (49,490) watched the homecoming contest.

Win No. 106

Florida State 66, Memphis State 17

November 17, 1979

1979 Season: 10-0

With rival Florida on the schedule the following week, many thought Florida State may look past the Tigers from Memphis. Bowden did not worry about motivation, as the Orange Bowl announced, just hours before the game, that the Seminoles would play in the annual classic. Bowden was not happy with a sluggish first quarter performance and benched several starters to start the second quarter. In response, Jordan threw touchdown passes to Flowers, Johnson, and King in an eight-minute span. During the second half, the defense got into the scoring with Piurowski intercepting a pass and returning it 29 yards for a score. Keith Jones added another touchdown when he recovered a blocked punt and returned it to the end zone.

Win No. 107

Florida State 27, Florida 16

November 23, 1979

1979 Season: 11-0

In front of a national television audience—the first in FSU history—the Seminoles beat their archrivals to cap their first undefeated regular season since Don Veller's squad went 8-0 in 1950. Leading at the half 10-0 on a Cappelen 42-yard field goal and a Johnson 21-yard touchdown catch, the 50-year-old Bowden told his team to be prepared for a hard fought second half. The Gators made it just that when they scored 10 points in the third quarter to tie the game. Woodham then replaced Jordan and orchestrated an 80-yard drive that ended when Lyles crashed up the middle for a 20-yard touchdown. A dramatic interception by tackle Walter Carter with under five minutes remaining set up Bill Capece's 18-yard field goal and a Florida State victory. Although Bowden's team ended the regular season undefeated, the Seminoles lost 21-7 in the Orange Bowl to Oklahoma and Heisman Trophy winner Billy Sims. Despite the setback, Florida State ended the year ranked sixth in the national polls.

YEAR FIFTEEN: THE 1980 SEASON (10–2)

Win No. 108
Florida State 16, Louisiana State 0
September 6, 1980
1980 Season: 1-0
A Top-10 finish the year before encouraged Seminole fans. In fact, at the conclusion of spring practice, there were 40,000 fans and a national television audience watching the Seminoles in the Garnet-and-Gold game. The Seminoles began the new year on the road in "Death Valley." Stellar defensive performances by seniors Ron Simmons and Monk Bonasorte led to the fourth shutout in Bowden's career at Florida State. Simmons, who was a consensus All American as a junior, began his senior season just as he had ended his 1979 campaign. In front of the third-largest crowd at Tiger Stadium, the future "Faarooq" with the World Wrestling Federation forced a fumble on the second play of the game. Cornerback Bobby Butler recovered the loose ball and Bill Capece ended a Seminole drive with a 34-yard field goal. The Seminoles, who forced another fumble on the Tigers' next possession, added another 34-yard field goal to lead 6-0 at halftime. Despite losing Simmons to a badly sprained ankle early in the second quarter, the Florida State defense continued to come up strong. In the third quarter, after Capece added another field goal to put the Seminoles up 9-0, Bonasorte intercepted a pass that set up wide receiver-turned-tailback Sam Platt's 3-yard touchdown to end the scoring for the game. With quarterback Rick Stockstill starting for the first time in his career, Bowden kept the ball on the ground as the 13th-ranked Seminoles ran the ball 57 times. The win pushed Bowden ahead of Tom Nugent into second place in school history with 35 FSU victories.

Win No. 109
Florida State 52, Louisville 0
September 13, 1980
1980 Season: 2-0
The Cardinals came to Tallahassee and were greeted rudely as they were held to 56 yards of total offense. The Seminole defense, while recording its second consecutive shutout, also scored when linebacker Ron Hester intercepted a pass and returned it 50 yards for a touchdown. However, unlike the win in the season opener, the Florida State defense was aided by an outstanding and balanced offensive effort. The Seminoles led 24-0 at halftime thanks to an offensive show by Stockstill and Platt. Stockstill had four touchdown passes and 115 yards. With backup quarterbacks Kelly Lowrey and Blair Williams each having a touchdown pass in the win, the Seminoles threw for a school-record 6 touchdowns. Dennis McKinnon was the favorite target with 6 receptions for 113 yards and 2 touchdowns.

All-American Ron Simmons (50) leads the team through stretches as Bowden looks on.

Win No. 110
Florida State 63, East Carolina 7
September 20, 1980
1980 Season: 3-0
The Florida State defense shut down the Pirates, but the shutout streak by the Seminoles came to an end when East Carolina's Anthony Collins returned a second-quarter kickoff 100 yards for a touchdown. As Bowden had done against LSU, he relied on his ground game to the tune of running the ball 81 times while calling 19 pass plays. The 100 offensive plays remain a team record for a single game. Against the Pirates, the ninth-ranked Seminoles scored in every quarter and racked up 336 rushing yards and 559 yards of total offense. With the win over East Carolina, the Seminoles had won 18 straight regular-season games. The streak would come to an end the next Saturday with a nail-biting, one-point loss to the Hurricanes at Miami. After a touchdown pass from Stockstill to tight end Sam Childers brought the Seminoles to 10-9 late in the fourth quarter, Bowden elected to go for a win instead of the tie. Miami ended Florida State's winning streak when noseguard Jim Burt broke up the attempted conversion.

Win No. 111
Florida State 18, Nebraska 14
October 4, 1980
1980 Season: 4-1

Coach Bowden ranks this victory over the Cornhuskers as one of his favorites. There are many reasons for him to look back at this win with fondness and awe. Florida State had to travel to Lincoln and play in front of a crowd of 76,152, the 108th consecutive sellout for the Cornhuskers. The Seminoles were facing a Nebraska squad that was undefeated and ranked third in the country. Editors from *Sports Illustrated* were so impressed with Nebraska's promising season that they had sent a writer to the game to cover how the Cornhuskers were on their way to a national championship. The Seminoles, coming off a heartbreaking loss to Miami in their previous game, had dropped out of the Top Ten. Despite the obstacles and the underdog status, the victory was secured by a defense that forced four second-half turnovers and a strong kicking game. The Florida State defense—spurred by an interception by Keith Jones, a forced fumble by Mark Macek, and a fumble recovery by Alphonso Carreker—held the Nebraska offensive juggernaut to 2 scores after it had been averaging 44 points a game. The biggest defensive stop came with 10 seconds remaining and the Cornhuskers 3 yards from a touchdown when linebacker Paul Piurowski crushed quarterback Jeff Quinn and forced the final turnover of the game. Bonasorte had another pick, which gave him a school record 13 career interceptions. After the Seminoles fell

Paul Piurowski crushed Nebraska's quarterback, giving FSU the ball and the victory.

behind 14-0 in the second quarter, the Seminoles scored 18 unanswered points to pull out the upset. Bill Capece hit four field goals, the last was a 41 yarder with 2:37 remaining. "A breakthrough win," Bowden later said. He commented in a post-game interview, "I would think this one is the all-time Seminole win."

Win No. 112
Florida State 36, Pittsburgh 22
October 11, 1980
1980 Season: 5-1
This win over the Panthers is another of Bowden's favorites. While it would be hard for the Seminoles to top their win a week earlier over Nebraska, the 11th-ranked Seminoles did their best with another upset of a 3rd-ranked powerhouse. This time, however, Florida State worked its magic in the friendly confines of Doak Campbell. Dan Marino was the star of the undefeated Panthers, but the Seminole defenders were the stars of the game as they forced Jackie Sherrill's team into 7 turnovers. A second-quarter offensive explosion pulled Florida State out of a 7-3 first-quarter deficit. Two touchdowns came when Stockstill hit Hardis Johnson for a 23-yard score and Sam Childers for a 4 yarder. Bill Capece, who had a total of 5 field goals in the game to set a school record, added field goals of 43 and 50 yards to put the Seminoles up 23-7 at halftime. In the second half Pittsburgh had two Marino-led rallies that closed the gap to 23-15 and 29-22. But the win was secured by 2 more field goals by Capece and a touchdown pass from Stockstill (his third of the game) to Kurt Unglaub. The Seminoles rushed for 163 yards against Hugh Green and a Pittsburgh defense that was ranked No. 1 in the nation against the run. The win in front of a record-setting crowd of 52,894 fans ended one of the best two-week runs in FSU history.

Win No. 113
Florida State 41, Boston College 7
October 18, 1980
1980 Season: 6-1
After facing two of the most formidable foes of any season, the Seminoles were happy to see a homecoming opponent on their schedule. In fact, they were so relieved to have a weaker opponent that they almost became disinterested in the game itself. "I was bored," Butler said in the locker room after the 35-point win. Butler's defensive teammates held the Eagles to 105 yards of total offense. The Florida State defense didn't allow any points and added 2 fumble recoveries, 2 interceptions (Reggie Herring and Jones), a safety, and a blocked punt that was returned by Hester for a touchdown. The only score by the Eagles came on an 83-yard interception return by Rich Dyer in the second quarter. Capece had four field goals (two in the first minute of the game) to give him 15 for a FSU single-season record.

Win No. 114
Florida State 24, Memphis State 3
October 25, 1980
1980 Season: 7-1
Platt, who rushed for a then school-record 188 yards on 29 carries against the Tigers, was

the focus of Bowden's game plan. Bowden, who has always found himself intrigued by the strategies involved in military conquests, exploited the weak rushing defense of Memphis State by running the ball for a season best 365 yards. The Seminoles had 455 yards of total offense. Stockstill directed the passing game with 90 yards including an 18-yard touchdown to Hardis Johnson. The touchdown pass put Florida State ahead 17-0 in the second quarter. A 3-yard touchdown run by fullback Mike Whiting (set up by Bobby Butler's blocked punt) in the third quarter increased the Seminoles' lead to 24-0.

Win No. 115
Florida State 45, Tulsa 2
November 1, 1980
1980 Season: 8-1
If a team could pull off the upset against the Seminoles, this was the week, as four previously unbeaten Top 25 teams (Alabama, UCLA, North Carolina, and Baylor) all were upset. Bowden, who had commented to a reporter that he was "scared to death, especially after the rash of upsets," relied on a balanced offense and a tough defense to ensure that there would be no surprises at home against Tulsa. The fifth-ranked Seminoles, led by Stockstill's 171 yards, scored in every quarter against the Golden Hurricane. Stockstill threw 2 touchdowns to put the Seminoles ahead 21-2 at halftime. Florida State doubled its point total in the third quarter with touchdown runs of 4 yards by Mike Whiting (his second of the game), 1 yard by Sam Platt, and 18 yards by Ricky Williams.

Win No. 116
Florida State 31, Virginia Tech 7
November 8, 1980
1980 Season: 9-1
With representatives from the Cotton, Sugar, and Orange Bowls in Tallahassee to assess Florida State's potential for a New Year's Day game, Bowden—who celebrated his 51st birthday on the day of the game—had his team working to perfection. "We knew we had to win," said Piurowski, "and win impressively for the bowl people." Initially, the Seminoles appeared lethargic on both sides of the ball. But a quick score by the Hokies jolted the Seminoles as they scored 31 unanswered points. Stockstill threw 2 second-quarter touchdowns to Johnson. The first came on a typical gamble by Bowden. With a Florida State drive stalled at the Virginia Tech 45, Bowden called for a bomb on a short fourth down play. The play call was perfect, as Virginia Tech blitzed and all Stockstill had to do was loft the ball to a streaking Johnson for a 45-yard score. A minute later—after Simmons recovered a fumble—Stockstill hit Johnson for an 11-yard touchdown to put the Seminoles up 14-7 at halftime. Florida State added 2 touchdown runs (by Stockstill and Platt) in the second half to secure the win. Platt had his school-record sixth 100-yard rushing game of the season with 108 yards. In addition to Simmons's fumble recovery, the defense intercepted 3 Virginia Tech passes and held the Hokies to 140 yards of total offense. Bill Capece ended the scoring with a 42-yard field goal in the fourth quarter. His score gave him 99 points on the season, breaking Penn State's Matt Bahr's two-year-old NCAA single-season points record.

Win No. 117

Florida State 17, Florida 13

December 6, 1980

1980 Season: 10-1

A national television audience witnessed a tale of two halves in the fourth consecutive win over the Gators. In the first half, the Seminoles struggled after a four-week layoff and fell behind 13-3. But from the beginning of the second half, the momentum shifted in favor of Florida State. Bowden, who was named the Bobby Dodd National Coach of the Year, told reporters after the game, "we came out in the third quarter and stuck it to them." On the first drive of the third quarter, the Seminoles went 82 yards with the last 19 yards coming on a touchdown pass from Stockstill to Johnson. The Seminoles went ahead for good on the second play of the fourth quarter with the second scoring connection (20 yards) between Stockstill and Johnson. The defense was particularly outstanding in the second half when it held the Gators to 31 yards. Five seniors, playing in their final home game, were very active in the win. Piurowski had 15 tackles and Herring added a fumble recovery and another 10 stops. Piurowski said to a reporter after the win, "I don't know how it would feel to win the World Series in four games, but I think it must feel like this." Jones had 2 key fourth-quarter interceptions, Butler had a first-half interception, and Bonasorte broke up 3 passes. With the win—in front of yet another record-setting crowd of 53,772 at Doak Campbell—the Seminoles ended the regular season ranked second in the nation. Florida State was then invited to its second consecutive Orange Bowl and suffered a heartbreaking 18-17 loss to wishbone quarterback J.C. Watts and his Oklahoma Sooners on New Year's Day. The loss dropped Florida State to fifth in the final polls.

YEAR SIXTEEN: THE 1981 SEASON (6–5)

Win No. 118

Florida State 17, Louisville 0

September 5, 1981

1981 Season: 1-0

Coach Bowden could only be excited when he saw the season-opening opponent. The Florida State coach had led back-to-back shutouts of the Cardinals in 1979 (27-0) and 1980 (52-0). Although the Seminoles were in a rebuilding year, FSU continued its shutout tradition over an outmatched Louisville squad. Just as the youthful defense dominated the game, first-year players led the Seminole offensive charge. In the first quarter, the host Seminoles went ahead 10-0 behind the efforts of two freshmen on back-to-back drives. Mike Rendina finished off the first drive when he hit a 24-yard field goal for the first points of the season. The other opening-quarter points came on Jessie Hester's 11-yard touchdown reception from Rick Stockstill. Florida State ended the scoring late in the fourth quarter when another freshman, Billy Allen, rushed for a 50-yard touchdown.

Punter Rohn Stark kept Memphis State out of good field position.

Win No. 119
Florida State 10, Memphis State 5
September 12, 1981
1981 Season: 2-0

The young Seminoles picked up their second home win in as many tries behind their stingy defense and exceptional special teams. While the defense allowed only a fourth-quarter field goal, punter Rohn Stark's 47-yard average kept the Tigers pinned in their own territory. The Florida State offense did just enough to give Bowden the win. Stockstill threw for 128 yards but was sacked for a safety in the first quarter. The Seminoles finally pulled ahead for good in the second quarter when Mike Whiting capped off a 76-yard drive with a 1-yard touchdown run. Rendina finished the Florida State scoring and secured the win with a 46-yard field goal in the fourth quarter.

Win No. 120
Florida State 36, Ohio State 27
October 3, 1981
1981 Season: 3-1

With one of the toughest traveling schedules in college football, the Seminoles had no time to rest as they faced one of their toughest challenges. They were on the road for their second of five consecutive road games against football powerhouses. This five-game swing earned Bowden the nicknames "King of the Road" and "Road Warrior" for his willingness to schedule road trips against the best teams in college football. Two weeks earlier, Florida State suffered its first loss of the year on the road at Nebraska. In Columbus, the Seminoles and Buckeyes changed leads throughout the first half. After an early Ohio State touchdown, Florida State jumped ahead with a field goal and a blocked punt that Ron

Hester recovered and returned for a 35-yard touchdown. The Seminoles went ahead again in the second quarter when Bowden called for a fake field goal. The play worked to perfection and Kelly Lowrey scored on a 5-yard run. Late in the second quarter, Florida State took the lead for good with Stockstill's 13-yard touchdown pass to Tony Johnson. Another touchdown throw by Stockstill (a 7 yarder to Sam Childers) came in the third quarter and put the Seminoles ahead 30-21. A few minutes later Ricky Williams added a 3-yard run to cap off the scoring for Florida State. Although Ohio State quarterback Art Schlichter threw for 458 yards, Stockstill had his career day by leading the Seminoles in the upset with his 299 yards and 2 passing touchdowns. Bowden considers this triumph and the victory over Notre Dame in the next game as two of his all-time favorites.

Win No. 121
Florida State 19, Notre Dame 13
October 10, 1981
1981 Season: 4-1
The Seminoles next visited South Bend hoping for their second consecutive upset on the road. It wasn't until Whiting caught a fourth-quarter 5-yard touchdown pass from Stockstill that Florida State could escape with the victory over the legendary team. A 17-yard scoring connection between Stockstill and Whiting had given the Seminoles their first lead of the game in the third quarter. While Whiting scored both touchdowns for Florida State, Williams continued his ground assault with 135 yards on 15 carries. Notre Dame could only muster 2 field goals over the first three quarters as the Irish had trouble moving against the Seminole defense. Florida State, while allowing a fourth-quarter touchdown run by Greg Bell, allowed only 38 yards through the air. This victory was meaningful to the young Seminoles and their coach, as Bowden had grown up listening to and idolizing the Irish legends. Bowden developed rheumatic fever as an early teenager and was confined to his home for 18 months. The youngster, who was bed-ridden for six months, listened to the radio where he immersed himself into the broadcasts of World War II and the football games played by Alabama and Notre Dame. As he said years later, "I was raised on Notre Dame." Although Knute Rockne passed away shortly after Bowden's birth, Bowden followed and tried to emulate other Notre Dame legends, including Frank Leahy. He also considers meeting Angelo Bertelli—the first Irish player to win the Heisman Trophy—one of his fondest memories. His listening to endless hours of radio broadcasts developed more than an interest in the football coaches and legends out of South Bend. It also had an impact on his coaching style, as he was forced to visualize the ongoing battles during WWI through the medium of the radio broadcasts. This action has a direct connection on Bowden's unique ability as a head coach to visualize several plays ahead.

Win No. 122
Florida State 38, Louisiana State 14
October 24, 1981
1981 Season: 5-2
The murderous five-state road trip, which had started in disappointment with the loss at Nebraska, ended on a high note with the sensational unveiling of Greg Allen and a

crushing defeat of the Tigers in Baton Rouge. For the third consecutive year, the LSU faithful were sent home disappointed after an upset by Florida State. In the contest, the Seminoles scored 17 first-quarter points and kept LSU at a safe distance throughout the remaining three quarters. Florida State, which started the scoring with a Rendina field goal, had a 17-0 lead after a touchdown through the air from Stockstill to Dennis McKinnon and a touchdown on the ground by Allen. The freshman tailback finished the game with 202 yards to become the first Florida State player to go over the 200-yard mark.

Win No. 123
Florida State 56, Western Carolina 31
October 31, 1981
1981 Season: 6-2
Allen obliterated the record books for the second consecutive week by rushing for 322 yards against the Catamounts. His yardage total destroyed his one-week old record and set the mark for the most yards in a game by a freshman running back. While his record would later be broken by several running backs including Marshall Faulk (386 yards in 1991) and Ron Dayne (339 in 1996), in the Florida State record books the next highest yardage total is Sammie Smith's 244-yard performance against East Carolina six years later. Allen, whose overall effort totaled 417 all-purpose yards, scored 2 touchdowns in the win. Florida State, scoring the most points of the season and the most since East Carolina in 1980, also got touchdowns from Whiting, McKinnon, Phil Williams, and Cedric Jones. The win was Bowden's 50th at FSU. But the Seminoles would go winless the rest of the season with

Bowden prepares his halftime speech.

losses to stars Jim Kelly (Miami), Sammy Winder (Southern Mississippi), and Wayne Peace (Florida).

YEAR SEVENTEEN: THE 1982 SEASON (9–3)

Win No. 124
Florida State 38, Cincinnati 31
September 4, 1982
1982 Season: 1-0

Although the Seminoles would not compete for a national championship, some sportswriters have suggested that Bowden coached his best season in 1982. After a 6-5 season in 1981, the prospects for a national ranking were slim. However, Bowden—along with his coaching staff that included sons Terry and Tommy serving as volunteer and part-time assistants—relied on an aggressive defense, a brilliant young running back, and a two-headed quarterback system to lead Florida State to another Top Ten finish. Bowden was worried that his players might overlook the Bearcats with No. 1 Pittsburgh coming to Tallahassee two weeks later. His fears were justified as the Seminoles fell behind 14-0 in the first quarter and had to squeak out a victory. The season opener would not have been as successful if not for the efforts of a player only known to the most ardent FSU followers. With Florida State leading 38-31 and only three minutes remaining, Cincinnati's Antonia

At his weekly press conference in 1982, Bowden answers questions about the season-opening win.

Gibson intercepted a pass from Florida State quarterback Blair Williams and appeared to be on his way for a possible winning touchdown. Out of nowhere FSU fullback Manny Carballo, who played most of previous season on the practice squad, caught Gibson at the 19-yard line to preserve the victory. Greg Allen scored 3 rushing touchdowns in the win.

Win No. 125
Florida State 24, Southern Mississippi 17
September 25, 1982
1982 Season: 2-1
Following a 37-17 loss to Pittsburgh, the visiting Seminoles beat the Golden Eagles on a fake field goal attempt. As the clock ticked down to under five minutes remaining, the two teams had battled to a 17-17 score. Bowden faced a fourth-and-goal from the 2-yard line. Most onlookers assumed that Bowden would kick the field goal and let his dominating defense secure the win. But Bowden did just the opposite. Phillip Hall lined up the kick, but holder Kelly Lowrey took the snap and used the quarterback keeper for the winning touchdown. The FSU defense—led by Ken Roe's 22 stops and Tommy Young's 21 tackles—then held the Golden Eagles to 7 yards on four plays on the last drive of the game.

Win No. 126
Florida State 34, Ohio State 17
October 2, 1982
1982 Season: 3-1
The Seminoles, just as they had done the previous year, traveled to Columbus and had little trouble with the Buckeyes. Bowden's offense impressed the 89,491 spectators with 476 yards of total offense. On the year FSU averaged 466 yards per game, ranking third in the country. Bowden took the Buckeyes by surprise early in the game. With the Seminoles behind 7-0 and on the Ohio State 11-yard line, Bowden once again made a little magic and history. Lowrey took the snap and pitched to Cedric Jones. Jones then threw to a wide-open Lowrey for a touchdown to give the Florida State offense a much-needed spark. As Bowden told reporters, Ohio State was "in man coverage and who doesn't get covered there? The quarterback." The halfback pass allowed Lowrey to become the first Seminole in school history to pass for a touchdown, run for another score, and catch a touchdown in a single game. Lowrey threw touchdowns to both Zeke Mowatt and Jessie Hester. His fourth-quarter connection with Hester—along with a 10-yard touchdown run by Ricky Williams—provided FSU with a comfortable lead.

Win No. 127
Florida State 59, Southern Illinois 8
October 9, 1982
1982 Season: 4-1
Homecoming games have typically been automatic wins for Bowden, as he did not lose one until his 26th season at Florida State. The Seminoles secured only a 21-yard field goal by Hall in the first quarter against the Salukis, but they scored four times in the second quarter to begin the rout. Bowden successfully used a two-quarterback system as Lowrey threw for

217 yards and 2 touchdowns and Blair Williams added 144 passing yards and 2 scores. Hester caught four passes for 94 yards and 2 touchdowns.

Win No. 128
Florida State 56, East Carolina 17
October 16, 1982
1982 Season: 5-1
Bowden preached all week about the strength and speed of the East Carolina defense. The Pirates were ranked in the Top-20 in fewest yards allowed. Lowrey, Allen, Blair Williams, and Cedric Jones were up to Bowden's challenge as they led the Seminoles to a school-record 706 yards in total offense. Allen scored 3 short touchdown runs and caught a 24-yard pass from Williams for another score. Jones, who would only rush for 167 yards in the season, led the way with 77 of the team's 250 yards on the ground. The Seminoles passed for 456 yards, led by Lowrey's 237 yards and Williams's 223 yards.

Win No. 129
Florida State 24, Miami 7
October 30, 1982
1982 Season: 6-1
The Hurricanes had a strong running game and announced to the media all week that they planned to continue running against Bowden's defense. Miami struggled on the ground as Roe, Young, David Ponder, Alphonso Carreker, and John McLean limited the Hurricanes to 91 rushing yards. Roe had 24 tackles while Young added 23. The two linebackers ended the season leading the Seminoles with 77 and 74 tackles, respectively. The Seminoles scored first on a 36-yard field goal by Hall. On the year, Hall connected on six-of-seven attempts prompting *Orlando Sentinel's* Brian Schmitz to write that the kicker "was perhaps the success story of the 1982 season." Allen capped a long, time-consuming drive with a leap over the defense from the three to put Florida State ahead 10-0 at halftime. The Hurricanes, stopped during one second-quarter drive on four consecutive plays inside the 6-yard line, finally found the end zone on a short touchdown run in the third quarter. Orson Mobley made a leaping 24-yard touchdown reception from Lowrey to give FSU a 17-7 lead. Allen then added a 2-yard run for the final score of the game.

Win No. 130
Florida State 56, South Carolina 26
November 6, 1982
1982 Season: 7-1
During the season, Allen set school records for season touchdowns (21), rushing touchdowns (20), and total points (126), all of which still stand. Four of his touchdowns and 173 rushing yards came against the Gamecocks. In addition to Allen's exploits on the ground, future NFL star Dennis McKinnon caught a perfectly thrown pass from Williams for an 83-yard score. Warren Hanna added another score by returning a blocked punt 28 yards for a touchdown late in the game. Once again Lowrey and Williams showed Bowden's two-quarterback system was effective as they passed for 269 and 168 yards, respectively.

Greg Allen set several rushing and scoring records during the 1982 season.

Win No. 131
Florida State 49, Louisville 14
November 17, 1982
1982 Season: 8-1
Doak Campbell was renovated before the season allowing 51,233 fans to watch Allen score four touchdowns for the second consecutive week. Although Allen would get the headlines with his touchdowns and 173 rushing yards, it was Ricky Williams who rushed for 140 yards and set up each of the scores. FSU's offense exploded with 615 total yards in front of a national television audience on WTBS. Gary Henry provided the most exciting play of the day as he scooped up a blocked punt and eluded several defenders on his way to a 42-yard touchdown. The win was followed by a loss on the road to Louisiana State and a home loss to Florida to end the regular season. Speculation about the retirement of Bear Bryant from Alabama led many to speculate that Bowden would soon be leaving Tallahassee. However, when Bryant stepped down in mid-December, Bowden made it clear that his future was with Florida State. While the Crimson Tide is currently on its sixth coach since Bryant, the Seminoles have had only one legendary leader in that time span.

Win No. 132 (Gator Bowl)
Florida State 31, West Virginia 12
December 30, 1982
1982 Season: 9-3
The Seminoles received a postseason invitation as a result of an impressive eight-win performance in the regular season. The Mountaineers were favored, but Bowden's defense rose to the occasion to defeat his former school. Before the game Bowden told reporters that

the heavy rain would favor the Mountaineers. But Allen, the bowl MVP, used the weather to his advantage as he raced for 138 yards and 2 touchdowns. Another Allen—Billy—electrified the fans as he returned a kickoff 95 yards for a score. As if the game was not exciting enough, McKinnon somersaulted after leaping high in the air to catch a pass by Williams for another score. Defensive backs Harvey Clayton, Larry Harris, and Ponder dominated WVU as they allowed only 10 completions by Jeff Hostetler. Bowden's Seminoles finished seventh in the final polls, marking the third time in four seasons that they were ranked in the Top Ten.

YEAR EIGHTEEN: THE 1983 SEASON (8–4)

Win No. 133
Florida State 47, East Carolina 46
September 3, 1983
1983 Season: 1-0
The Pirates traveled to Tallahassee as huge underdogs. But in a game that featured eight lead changes, the Seminoles finally secured the win with a fumble recovery and interception by Eric Riley and 2 second-half touchdown passes by Kelly Lowrey. Lowrey and tailback Greg Allen led the highly productive Seminole offense. Twelve months earlier Lowrey was a third stringer on the quarterback depth chart. But during the 1983 spring practice, his status improved so significantly that Bowden commented to reporters, "how Lowrey goes, so goes the Seminole offense." The senior ended the game completing 28 passes for 322 yards and 3 touchdowns. Allen continued his prolific offensive charge with 3 rushing touchdowns and 154 yards on the ground.

Bowden leads the Seminoles on the field.

Win No. 134

Florida State 40, Louisiana State 35

September 10, 1983

1983 Season: 2-0

After falling behind by 2 touchdowns, the 12th-ranked Seminoles came roaring back with 33 unanswered points to pull out the road win in front of a record-setting crowd at Tiger Stadium. Because of a missed field goal and a lost fumble, the Seminoles found themselves behind 14-0 in the first quarter. But Lowrey scored his second of 2 quarterback-sneak touchdowns on the last play of the first half to even the score. Lowrey ended the game with 233 yards and 5 touchdowns (2 passing and 3 rushing). Allen, who had 201 rushing yards, added 3 more touchdowns in the third and early fourth quarters to put Florida State up 33-14. The teams then exchanged scores before the Seminole defense allowed 2 late scores by the Tigers that made the game appear much closer than it actually was.

Win No. 135

Tulane 34, Florida State 28 (forfeit)

September 17, 1983

1983 Season: 3-0

Bowden's Seminoles traveled to New Orleans ranked ninth in the country. His players fell behind by 2 touchdowns early and were upset by quarterback John English and the Green Wave. Although English threw for 210 yards and a touchdown, the NCAA had declared him ineligible to play. His father, Wally English, had played his son anticipating he would be reinstated. English wasn't reinstated and Tulane was forced to forfeit the win. Florida State was fortunate to get the forfeit, as the team struggled with sickness and costly mistakes. The offense was limited as Lowrey had been sick all week and Allen sprained his knee in the third quarter. The Seminoles also committed four turnovers and allowed a long punt return for a touchdown.

Win No. 136

Florida State 43, Cincinnati 17

October 15, 1983

1983 Season: 4-2

Bowden was inducted into the Florida Sport Hall of Fame in 1983. In just his eighth season in Tallahassee, Bowden beat the Bearcats and surpassed Bill Peterson to become Florida State's all-time leader in coaching victories with 63 wins. After being on the road for four consecutive weeks, including back-to-back losses at Auburn and Pittsburgh, the Seminoles were happy to be at Doak Campbell. Florida State jumped out to a 16-0 lead in the first quarter, with the first score coming when offensive lineman Herbert Harp recovered a fumble in the end zone. Despite the big lead, it took 2 fourth-quarter touchdowns on a 4-yard run by Allen and a 29-yard scoring connection between backup quarterback Bob Davis and Jessie Hester to secure the win. Allen and fellow tailback Roosevelt "Rosie" Snipes led Florida State's impressive 304-yard rushing attack with 125 and 121 yards, respectively.

Although he prefers sunshine, Bowden's teams have also excelled in rainy conditions.

Win No. 137

Florida State 51, Louisville 7

October 20, 1983

1983 Season: 5-2

Florida State played its first Thursday night contest when Bowden agreed to switch the game against the Cardinals from its scheduled Saturday start in order to accommodate the wishes of Superstation WTBS. Florida State put on an offensive show for the home crowd and national television audience, racking up 545 yards of total offense and allowing only a fourth-quarter score by Louisville. The Seminoles led 28-0 at halftime behind a 45-yard touchdown pass from Lowrey to Hester, 2 touchdown runs by Allen, and a rushing score by Snipes. Florida State continued their offensive assault in the second half. The Seminoles built a 51-0 lead, with Allen, Pete Panton, and 25-year-old ex-serviceman Billy Allen all seeing the end zone. Greg Allen ended the game with 145 yards and 3 rushing touchdowns. The defense held the Cardinals to 49 yards passing and one fourth-quarter score.

Win No. 138

Florida State 29, Arizona State 26

October 29, 1983

1983 Season: 6-2

With six seconds left in the game, Davis hit Hester for a 10-yard touchdown to give the Seminoles the win at Sun Devil Stadium. Davis, who stepped in when Lowrey was sidelined with a fourth-quarter knee injury, engineered the game-winning drive from the Florida State 18. For the game, Davis completed only 8 passes but 2 of his completions went for touchdowns. Earlier in the fourth quarter, he hit Snipes on a 38-yard score. Sun Devils coach Daryl Rogers was so impressed with Bowden's offense that he told reporters, "Florida State's offense was the best I've ever coached against." The Seminoles ended the game with 252 yards on the ground and 218 passing yards.

Win No. 139

Florida State 45, South Carolina 30

November 5, 1983

1983 Season: 7-2

In a game in which Bowden said his players "outslopped the world," two reserves led the Seminoles to a come-from-behind victory over the traveling Gamecocks. After South Carolina built a 24-17 lead in the third quarter, Davis directed four scoring drives, including 2 touchdown passes, to give FSU the win. Snipes, who ran for 106 yards of Florida State's 298 rushing yards, scored 2 touchdowns in the third quarter. His first touchdown on an 18-yard run broke a 24-24 deadlock. Florida State extended its lead on the next drive when Snipes hauled in an 8-yard touchdown pass from Davis. The Seminoles ended their scoring in the fourth quarter when Davis hit Weegie Thompson for a 36-yard touchdown. FSU ended the regular season with back-to-back losses to Miami and Florida.

Win No. 140 (Peach Bowl)

Florida State 28, North Carolina 3

December 30, 1983

1983 Season: 8-4

In his seventh bowl, Bowden relied on a hot new signal caller and an outstanding defensive performance to pull out the win in Atlanta. Third-year sophomore Eric Thomas, an oft-injured quarterback who was making his first career start, was on fire as he led 2 scoring drives in the first quarter. His opening drive ended when he found Weegie Thompson for a 15-yard touchdown. On his second possession, he again capped off a drive by hitting Thompson for an 18-yard score. Bowden then relied on his ground game to defeat the Tar Heels. The Seminoles, who ran for 265 yards, added to their lead and went into halftime ahead 21-0 with a 1-yard touchdown run by Snipes after Pete Panton recovered a fumble. Thomas led a game-ending drive that he finished with a 1-yard touchdown run. Tackle Alphonso Carreker led a defensive effort that held the Tar Heels to 32 yards on the ground and 166 yards through the air. Carreker was named the defensive MVP while Thomas won the offensive MVP award.

YEAR NINETEEN: THE 1984 SEASON (7-3-2)

Win No. 141

Florida State 48, East Carolina 17

September 1, 1984

1984 Season: 1-0

The Seminoles—loaded with such talent as Greg Allen, Jessie Hester, and Jamie Dukes—were again explosive through the air and on the ground, ending the year ranked fourth in the nation in total offense. In the season opener, a 21-point outburst in the second quarter quickly put away the Pirates. Throughout his career, Bowden often used the reverse to surprise opponents and thrill the fans. On this day the fans in Tallahassee were given a special treat as Darrin Holloman scored twice on reverses. With Dukes providing the protection, Eric Thomas had the time to throw a 31-yard touchdown strike to Hester.

Thomas completed 12 passes for 177 yards and Allen ran for 113 yards in leading the 327-yard rushing attack by the Seminoles.

Win No. 142
Florida State 42, Kansas 16
September 15, 1984
1984 Season: 2-0
With FSU leading Kansas 21-10 late in the third quarter, Joe Wessel and the Seminole punt defense took center stage. Attempting to punt for the Jayhawks, Tom Becker mishandled the snap, allowing the fleet-footed Wessel to sack the punter and giving the visiting Seminoles the ball on the Kansas 15-yard line. Allen then broke several tackles to reach the end zone and Florida State led 28-10. After the Jayhawks ran three plays with no gain, Becker attempted another punt. This time Wessel blocked the kick and Bruce Heggie scored from the seven to put the game out of reach. Allen (134 yards) and Cletis Jones (114 yards) each scored twice on the ground.

Win No. 143
Florida State 38, Miami 3
September 22, 1984
1984 Season: 3-0
Visiting the defending national champions proved to be no problem for the Seminoles. While Derek Schmidt and Hester provided the offensive excitement, the defense shut

Joe Wessel re-wrote the record book with five blocked kicks and four blocked punts in 1984.

down the explosive Hurricane offense. Florida State sacked Bernie Kosar 6 times and limited future NFL stars Kosar and Vinny Testaverde to 237 passing yards. Henry Taylor and Fred Jones led the defense. The linebackers finished the season leading the Seminoles in tackles with 80 and 65, respectively. Schmidt kicked field goals of 54, 40, and 38 yards to account for the only scoring in the first half. Unable to gain any momentum on the first possession of the second half, FSU faced a third-and-17 and Bowden again used his pet play to perfection. Hester took a reverse to the left and outran the entire defense for a 77-yard touchdown. Rosie Snipes later added 2 touchdowns to complete the scoring.

Win No. 144
Florida State 44, Temple 27
September 29, 1984
1984 Season: 4-0
Wessel—for the second time in three games—was incredible on special teams; he became only the second Seminole to block 2 kicks in one game. His first exploit came in the first half when he leaped high to block a punt that was recovered by John Eaford at the Temple 44-yard line. On the ensuing drive, Florida State forced a third-and-28. Most assumed Bowden would try a long pass to the end zone. Instead, Bowden ran a draw with Allen, who went virtually untouched for a score. Minutes later, Wessel blocked a field goal attempt that Eric Riley grabbed and raced 40 yards for another FSU touchdown.

Win No. 145
Florida State 27, Tulane 6
October 20, 1984
1984 Season: 5-1-1
Coming off a tie at Memphis State and a one-point home loss to Auburn, Bowden relied on his special teams to once again win a contest. Although Wessel did not block a kick this game, he recovered Lenny Chavers's blocked kick and took it 10 yards for a touchdown to break a 6-6 deadlock late in the third quarter. After stopping Tulane on three plays, the Seminoles forced another Green Wave punt. This time Jesse Solomon blocked the kick and recovered it in the end zone for a score. Allen provided the final points when he dashed 42 yards to the end zone.

Win No. 146
Florida State 52, Arizona State 44
November 3, 1984
1984 Season: 6-1-1
The Sun Devils were aware of Wessel; they just couldn't stop him. Trailing 17-0 in the second quarter, Florida State again turned to the special teams for a spark. Chavers ignited the Seminoles when he blocked a punt that Wessel returned for a score. After each team made long field goals, Kirk Coker replaced an injured Thomas and led FSU to a touchdown just before the half. Following 2 long Florida State touchdowns (an 81-yard Allen run and a 69-yard Coker-to-Hester pass), Wessel struck again. This time he blocked a punt and recovered it going 34 yards for his second touchdown. Wessel's 2 scores off blocks are still

an FSU record. His 5 blocked kicks on the season and FSU's 8 blocks on the year also remain as school marks. While Allen rushed for 223 yards, his season came to an end when he suffered a knee injury late in the game.

Win No. 147
Florida State 37, Tennessee-Chattanooga 0
November 17, 1984
1984 Season: 7-2-1
With the injury to Allen in the Arizona State game, Bowden knew his hopes for a New Year's Day bowl were lost. Following a 38-26 loss at South Carolina, Bowden returned to Tallahassee for the annual homecoming game. Florida State—led by Taylor's 12 tackles— shut out the Moccasins while limiting them to 165 yards of total offense. The Seminoles compiled 618 yards on offense, getting 2 scores and 151 yards from Snipes, 1 touchdown and 117 yards from Hester, and 1 score and 111 yards from Cletis Jones. Hester's touchdown came on a 47-yard pass from Coker. The Seminoles rushed for 454 yards and passed for 164 yards to set a school record as the most lopsided (290 yards) offensive output in favor of rushing. Despite a home loss to Florida two weeks later, Florida State was still invited to postseason play, where the Seminoles came back from a two-touchdown deficit to tie Georgia 17-17 in the Citrus Bowl. Wessel scored the final points of the game on a 14-yard return of a kick blocked by Chavers.

Bowden meets with the media before the Citrus Bowl.

YEAR TWENTY: THE 1985 SEASON (9–3)

Win No. 148
Florida State 38, Tulane 12
August 31, 1985
1985 Season: 1-0
Bowden began his 10th season at Florida State in the New Orleans Superdome. Danny McManus, who completed only 5 passes as a redshirt freshman in 1984, had an outstanding game with 2 rushing and 2 passing touchdowns to give Bowden his 75th win at FSU. McManus, whose opportunity came after Eric Thomas could not come back from shoulder surgery, won the starting position by edging out Kirk Coker in spring practice. Concussions eventually sidelined McManus, opening the door for three other Seminoles who started games during the season. Freshman Chip Ferguson eventually emerged as the team's starter. But against the Green Wave, it was all McManus as he threw touchdown passes to Phillip Bryant and Darrin Holloman to give Florida State a 14-12 halftime lead. In the second half—behind two 1-yard touchdown runs by McManus, a 49-yard field goal by Derek Schmidt, and another 14-yard score by fullback Cletis Jones—the Seminoles blew open the game by scoring 24 unanswered points.

Win No. 149
Florida State 17, Nebraska 13
September 7, 1985
1985 Season: 2-0
Bowden looks back with great fondness on this upset win before a national television audience. His 17th-ranked Seminoles traveled to Lincoln and came away with a defensive-led victory over the 10th-ranked Cornhuskers. Nebraska completed only 3 passes in the game and was held scoreless in the second half. Down 7-0 in the first quarter, McManus tied the game with a 4-yard touchdown pass to Holloman. Schmidt's 20-yard field goal early in the second quarter gave Florida State a 10-7 lead. Nebraska retook the lead on a 1-yard run by Doug DuBose, but FSU went into halftime ahead 17-13 when Cletis Jones scored on a 2-yard run. Garth Jax had set up the touchdown run when he sacked the punter on the Cornhusker 7-yard line. The FSU defense—led by Paul McGowan's 14 tackles, Greg Newell's 13 stops, and Fred Jones's 13 tackles—shut out the vaunted Nebraska offense in the second half. Martin Mayhew and Deion Sanders closed the passing lanes as the Cornhuskers were held to 40 yards passing. One of the biggest plays of the year came when McGowan stopped a fourth-quarter drive with an interception. McGowan's overall effort resulted in his winning Defensive Player of the Week honors from *Sports Illustrated* and the *Associated Press*. The Cornhuskers had one last drive left in them, but it ended when the Seminole defenders held strong on a fourth-down play to end the game.

Win No. 150
Florida State 19, Memphis State 10
September 21, 1985
1985 Season: 3-0
Another national television audience witnessed this win. Bowden said before the season that "it will be extremely important for us to get off to a good start. Our first three games will be seen coast-to-coast and that will set the stage for the rest of the year." Although Bowden had to rely on four field goals by Schmidt to pick up his 150th career win, he was thrilled with the come-from-behind victory in front of nearly 55,000 spectators at Doak Campbell and thousands more on television. Bowden did leave the game uncertain about the quarterback position, as McManus suffered his second concussion in as many games. Tony Smith, one of eight different players to line up at running back during the season, led all rushers with 18 carries for 96 yards. Alphonso Williams had a key third-quarter interception and his Florida State defenders held their opponent scoreless in the second half for the third consecutive week.

Win No. 151
Florida State 24, Kansas 20
September 28, 1985
1985 Season: 4-0
With the visiting Jayhawks leading 20-10 in the fourth quarter, the Seminoles needed a miracle, come-from-behind victory. In stepped Ferguson, who, on his second play of the

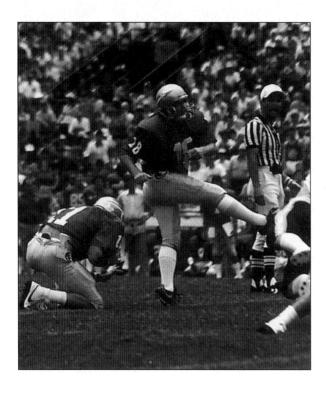

Derek Schmidt single-handedly outscored Memphis State.

season, hit Bryant with a 67-yard touchdown pass that brought the Seminoles to within a
field goal. Mayhew's interception, one of 3 second-half pickoffs by the Seminole defense,
gave Ferguson the ball again. Victor Floyd, who had just completed a 32-yard run, capped
off Ferguson's second drive by running 6 yards for the game-winning score.

Win No. 152
Florida State 76, Tulsa 14
October 19, 1985
1985 Season: 5-1
The Seminoles, coming off a loss to Bo Jackson's Auburn Tigers, returned home and gave
their fans a show with 11 touchdowns against the Golden Hurricane. Thomas threw first-
half touchdown passes to Pat Carter and Hassan Jones while Ferguson hit Jones once and
Bryant twice for second-half scores. The most electrifying moment came in the fourth
quarter when a 6-foot-1, 175-pound freshman defensive back from North Ft. Myers
brought the 53,500 fans to their feet with a school-record 100-yard interception return
for Florida State's final touchdown of the game. That freshman was none other than
Deion Sanders.

*Deion Sanders set the school
record with a 100-yard
interception return.*

Win No. 153
Florida State 20, North Carolina 10
October 26, 1985
1985 Season: 6-1
All season long, wins had been secured or preserved by interceptions by the Florida State defense. With the Seminoles holding to a slim 13-10 lead and the Tar Heels driving, Mayhew came through again by intercepting a pass and returning it 62 yards for a touchdown with 50 seconds remaining to give Bowden the victory. Florida State secured its first lead with 2:17 remaining on Schmidt's 51-yard field goal. Ferguson again came in as a second-half replacement and immediately led the Seminoles to their only offensive. His 10-yard scoring connection with Hassan Jones tied the game at 10. FSU's drive for a possible national championship came to an end on a 35-27 loss to Miami the following week.

Win No. 154
Florida State 56, South Carolina 14
November 9, 1985
1985 Season: 7-2
Bowden turned 56 the day before the game, but Florida State was in no mood to celebrate. The Seminoles had revenge on their minds, as their hopes for a major bowl in 1984 had been dashed when the Gamecocks pulled off an upset in Columbia. Back at home and in front of a national ESPN audience, the Seminoles had little trouble finding the end zone. Ferguson threw 3 touchdowns and scored on a 1-yard keeper. True freshman Keith Ross had 163 yards and 2 touchdowns. Floyd added 15 carries for 212 yards and 2 touchdowns in the blowout.

Win No. 155
Florida State 50, Western Carolina 10
November 16, 1985
1985 Season: 8-2
The Seminoles continued their rushing assault, racking up 379 yards and 5 touchdowns on the ground. For this homecoming game against the Catamounts, Tony Smith led all runners with 114 yards. Ross added another 103 yards and 2 rushing touchdowns. Floyd and Chuck Wells each had short touchdown runs in the second half. Ferguson directed the offense and had 182 yards passing, including a 10-yard second-quarter touchdown pass to All-American Hassan Jones.

Win No. 156 (Gator Bowl)
Florida State 34, Oklahoma State 23
December 30, 1985
1985 Season: 9-3
With Bowden's top three wide receivers out of action and an extremely impressive regular season running attack, few could blame the Cowboys for assuming that he would rely on his ground game. However, he fooled everyone by calling pass plays on 15 of the first 20 plays. The game ended with Ferguson winning the MVP award after completing 20-of-43 passes

Chip Ferguson was the MVP of the 1985 Gator Bowl.

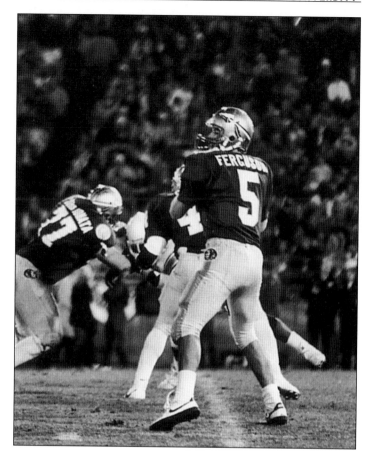

for 338 yards and 2 touchdowns. The Seminoles took a 13-0 halftime lead behind 2 Schmidt field goals and a 39-yard touchdown pass from Ferguson to Herb Gainer. Gainer caught 7 passes for 148 yards and 2 touchdowns. Ferguson's second touchdown came in the third quarter when he found Gainer for a 19-yard score to put the Seminoles ahead 27-3. When the Cowboys pulled to within 10 points, Ferguson responded with a 1-yard keeper in the fourth quarter to seal the win. Bowden didn't abandon the run as the Seminoles had 231 rushing yards with Tony Smith carrying the ball 24 times for 201 yards.

YEAR TWENTY-ONE: THE 1986 SEASON (7-4-1)

Win No. 157
Florida State 24, Toledo 0
August 30, 1986
1986 Season: 1-0
Beginning his second decade with the Seminoles, Bowden, while coaching a young team that faced three top-five opponents, directed Florida State to a fifth straight bowl. In the season opener at home against the Rockets, the defense, led by Fred Jones and Gerald

Chip Ferguson (5) led FSU to an early lead in the season opener.

Nichols, secured Bowden's first shutout in two years. The offense had trouble holding onto the ball with turnovers in each of the first three possessions. Chip Ferguson eventually engineered three first-half scoring drives. The first ended with Derek Schmidt's 24-yard field goal. The Seminoles went ahead 17-0 at halftime following second-quarter touchdown runs by Dayne Williams and David Palmer. FSU had back-to-back turnovers to open the second half and were held scoreless until Peter Tom Willis entered in the fourth quarter and led a 78-yard drive that was capped by a touchdown pass to Herb Gainer.

Win No. 158
Florida State 54, Tulane 21
October 11, 1986
1986 Season: 2-2-1
The Seminoles had just completed a tough, three-game stretch in which they lost at Nebraska, tied North Carolina in Tallahassee, and lost at Michigan. The game against the Wolverines gave Danny McManus valuable playing time as he rallied the Seminoles to within two points. His performance earned him his first start in a year. Against the Green Wave, he scored the first points of the game on a 1-yard touchdown sneak. On Tulane's next possession, Felton Hayes intercepted a pass and ran it back for a 20-yard score. McManus then led the offense to scores in each of its possessions in the third quarter. During the second-half rout, Victor Floyd, Tanner Holloman, Sammie Smith, Keith Ross, and Dexter Carter each scored a touchdown.

Danny McManus listens as Bowden calls a play.

Win No. 159
Florida State 59, Wichita State 3
October 18, 1986
1986 Season: 3-2-1
McManus led such a scoring assault on the Shockers that no one would be surprised if his performance didn't contribute to Wichita State's decision to eliminate its football program a few weeks later. Playing only the first half, McManus engineered 6 scoring drives while throwing for 201 yards and 3 scores. Six different Seminoles found the end zone, including 2 touchdown receptions by Ronald Lewis and 2 touchdown runs by Palmer. Bowden attempted to have mercy on the Shockers by playing all of his eligible players, including 11 running backs and 4 quarterbacks. Paul McGowan, who led the Seminoles on defense, finished the season as the school leader in tackles for the second consecutive year.

Win No. 160
Florida State 54, Louisville 18
October 25, 1986
1986 Season: 4-2-1
Bowden's offense continued to roll up points as McManus led the Seminoles to their third consecutive game of over 50 points. That streak was the first for a team from Florida. McManus threw for 3 first-half touchdowns and ran for a third-quarter score in the blowout. Gainer added 2 first-half touchdown receptions. Florida State had a commanding 34-7 lead in the second quarter behind a field goal, Gainer's 2 scores, and touchdowns by

Darrin Holloman, Dayne Williams, and Victor Floyd. Floyd had 110 yards rushing as Bowden relied on a strong running game (62 carries for 350 yards) on a rainy evening against Howard Schnellenberger's Cardinals.

Win No. 161
Florida State 45, South Carolina 28
November 8, 1986
1986 Season: 5-3-1
A week earlier, against Miami, Bowden made a call that resulted in one of the most exciting plays of the season. Keith Ross caught a kickoff and returned it 10 yards before stopping and firing the ball across the field to Dexter Carter. The freshman then found a line of blockers who opened the way for a 90-yard touchdown run. Despite the brilliant play calling, the Seminoles suffered their third loss of the season. Florida State appeared headed for disaster

Dayne Williams scored touchdowns against Louisville and South Carolina.

the next week at Williams-Brice Stadium as the Seminoles fell behind 21-6 late in the second quarter. Bowden—on his 57th birthday—was despondent with his quarterback situation, as McManus had an injured thumb and Willis was rendered ineffective after being rattled by the blitzing Gamecocks. Ferguson entered the game late in the second quarter and led the come-from-behind effort. After Ferguson hit Victor Floyd for a 24-yard score to pull FSU to within 21-13 at halftime, Floyd and Williams each ran for 2 touchdowns to lead the Seminoles in a 29-point, third-quarter explosion.

Win No. 162
Florida State 49, Southern Mississippi 13
November 15, 1986
1986 Season: 6-3-1
Bowden—who was inducted into the Alabama Sports Hall of Fame in 1986—secured Florida State's fifth straight bowl appearance and improved to 11-0 in homecoming games at FSU with the win over the Golden Eagles. The game provided Bowden with a chance to rest his starters and give his talented second and third teams plenty of playing time. Seven different players scored a touchdown and eleven players ran the ball, led by freshman Sammie Smith's 74 yards on only four carries. Ten Seminoles had at least 1 reception. Eric Williams had 2 interceptions, including one he returned 51 yards for a third-quarter score.

Win No. 163 (All-American Bowl)
Florida State 27, Indiana 13
December 31, 1986
1986 Season: 7-4-1
The Seminoles returned to Bowden's Birmingham roots to play the Hoosiers. In the history of FSU football, the bowl victory over Indiana is very insignificant compared to the decision made by Bowden after the game. Throughout December, the University of Alabama had courted Bowden with the hopes that the legendary coach would return to his home state and lead the Crimson Tide back to the glory it had during the years of Bowden's hero, Bear Bryant. Bowden was tempted to leave FSU, especially after a devastating and wet home loss to Florida—the sixth straight loss to the Gators—in the last game of the regular season. In fact, Bowden still ranks the 1986 loss to Florida as one of the worst memories of his coaching career. In addition to the Florida loss, the overall season was not kind to Bowden as he tried to recover from major setbacks. Off the field, Bowden was shaken by the shooting death of offensive tackle Pablo Lopez. On the field, Bowden's team suffered a tie against the Tar Heels and away losses to the Cornhuskers, Wolverines, and Hurricanes. But Bowden, who saw a glimpse of his future with Florida State after bowl MVP Sammie Smith rushed for 205 yards and 2 touchdowns against Indiana, discussed the potential move with Ann Bowden on the drive back from the bowl game. It's not a surprise he consulted Ann—his wife of 54 years—because he states that she, the Christian Church, and his parents have had the greatest influence on his life. When they arrived home, he announced to reporters gathered in his driveway that the Bowdens would remain in Tallahassee. That historic decision changed the course of Florida State football history, as his Seminoles—starting in 1987—would do something no school has ever done: by finishing among the AP

Top Five for 14 consecutive seasons. The 1987 season would be the start of the Bowden dynasty as he would lead the Seminoles to 14 consecutive 10-win seasons. Additionally, the heartbreaking loss to the Gators in 1986 would be the last time Florida State would suffer a home loss to Florida.

Raising helmets and walking to the end zone are a pre-game tradition at Florida State University.

PART IV

THE BOWDEN DYNASTY

FLORIDA STATE UNIVERSITY (1987–PRESENT)

WINS 164–332

YEAR TWENTY-TWO: THE 1987 SEASON (11–1)

Win No. 164

Florida State 40, Texas Tech 16

September 5, 1987

1987 Season: 1-0

There was great optimism for the 1987 season as the Seminoles returned 18 starters and 42 of their top 50 players. Even Bowden, who entered the season fourth among active coaches in wins, noted before the first game that his team had "the potential to challenge for a national championship." His experienced squad, while unable to win it all, did start the best winning streak over a 14-year period in the history of intercollegiate football. The first win came at home against the Red Raiders in Bowden's 11th consecutive season-opening victory. With Burt Reynolds present after having a football dorm named in his honor, the Seminoles rolled up 507 yards of offense behind Danny McManus. The fifth-year senior had a touchdown run and 2 passing scores while throwing for a career-high 275 yards.

Win No. 165

Florida State 44, East Carolina 3

September 12, 1987

1987 Season: 2-0

Sammie Smith had his regular-season breakout game after missing the season opener with a sprained knee. The heralded sophomore's performance in the All-American Bowl, after two years of injuries and adjustments, led to high expectations for the tailback. Smith didn't let anyone down as he rushed for 244 yards. His 83-yard touchdown run in the second quarter broke open a 6-3 game. McManus had a 59-yard touchdown pass to Randy White, and Chip Ferguson led 2 scoring drives in the fourth quarter.

Win No. 166

Florida State 41, Memphis State 24

September 19, 1987

1987 Season: 3-0

McManus led three long drives in the first quarter that resulted in two 1-yard touchdown runs by Dayne Williams and a 4-yard rushing score by Dexter Carter. Florida State needed the 21-0 first-quarter cushion, as 6 FSU turnovers enabled the Tigers to remain within striking distance. Carter had the most all-purpose yards for a Seminole in six years with 135 yards rushing, 63 yards receiving, and 113 yards on four kickoff returns. Ronald Lewis had 5 receptions for 107 yards. The Seminoles compiled 533 yards for their third consecutive 500-yard game. Paul McGowan led the defense with 16 tackles.

Win No. 167
Florida State 31, Michigan State 3
September 26, 1987
1987 Season: 4-0
Heisman Trophy candidate Lorenzo White received the pre-game publicity, but it was Bowden's play calling that stole the show. The Seminoles, who opened with Lawrence Dawsey's 23-yard reverse on the first play of the game, ran a total of five reverses with Lewis running three. His third-quarter reverse went for 56 yards and a touchdown that broke open a 7-3 Florida State lead. The Seminole defense, led by McGowan (14 tackles) and future FSU assistant coach Odell Haggins (14 tackles, including 2 sacks), held White to 84 yards and allowed only four completed passes. Haggins ended the year with 73 tackles and 8 sacks. Cornerbacks Eric Williams and Deion Sanders had big games as Williams blocked a third-quarter punt and Sanders intercepted a pass in the fourth quarter.

*Deion Sanders returns
an interception.*

Win No. 168

Florida State 61, Southern Mississippi 10

October 10, 1987

1987 Season: 5-1

The Seminoles suffered a devastating 26-25 loss to Miami seven days earlier. In fact, Bowden still ranks the loss to the Hurricanes as one of his worst memories of coaching. His Seminoles took out their frustrations for the loss on the Golden Eagles. Bowden played his starters sparingly as 11 players caught a pass and 8 had at least one carry. Smith led all rushers with 142 yards. McManus, Ferguson, and Peter Tom Willis each threw a touchdown pass as the Seminoles had 602 yards on offense. Kelvin Smith blocked 2 punts and Stan Shiver had 2 of Florida State's 5 interceptions.

Win No. 169

Florida State 32, Louisville 9

October 17, 1987

1987 Season: 6-1

The Seminoles had another explosive day compiling 542 yards against the Cardinals. Florida State had 349 rushing yards as Smith earned his third consecutive 100-yard game with 119 yards and a first-quarter 45-yard fake reverse for a touchdown. Victor Floyd led all rushers with 142 yards. The Seminoles took a 17-3 lead on a touchdown pass from McManus to Herb Gainer that was set up by an Alphonso Williams's blocked punt. The defense held the Cardinals to 27 rushing yards.

Win No. 170

Florida State 73, Tulane 14

October 31, 1987

1987 Season: 7-1

The Green Wave scored first following a turnover by the Seminoles, but Florida State went on to score 9 unanswered touchdowns to destroy Mack Brown and his squad. FSU, which led 38-7 at halftime, had its second 600-yard offensive performance on the season with 604 yards. Smith led all rushers with 111 yards and receivers with 87 yards. Smith and Dayne Williams each scored 3 touchdowns. Sanders, who had his third interception of the season while holding the then NCAA all-time receiving yardage leader Marc Zeno to four receptions, had his second career punt return for a touchdown during Florida State's 28-point third quarter.

Win No. 171

Florida State 34, Auburn 6

November 7, 1987

1987 Season: 8-1

The sixth-ranked Seminoles went on the road to face the fourth-ranked Tigers. Bowden ranks this win among his top coaching memories. The members of the 1985 freshman class put on a show to help FSU pull off the huge upset. Florida State's offense rolled and its defense forced 6 turnovers. McManus, who threw 3 touchdowns in the win, engineered 5 scoring drives in the first half as FSU went into halftime ahead 27-3. Pat Carter had a career day for a Florida State tight end, catching 7 passes for 79 yards and a touchdown. Terry Warren's 2 fumble recoveries and Stan Shiver's key second-quarter interception led the defense. A national television audience witnessed Derek Schmidt—FSU's place-kicker for a fourth consecutive season—win the CBS player of the game honor as he became the all-time NCAA scoring leader.

Win No. 172
Florida State 41, Furman 10
November 14, 1987
1987 Season: 9-1
Sammie Smith responded after the Paladins scored early. The Seminoles put on a balanced offensive show (243 yards rushing; 200 yards passing) for the Doak Campbell fans and Fiesta Bowl representatives who were on hand. Smith, who had the second-longest run in school history when he ran for a 95-yard touchdown in the third quarter, had 176 yards rushing for his sixth 100-yard game on the season. The Seminoles finished their scoring in the fourth quarter with a 12-yard rushing touchdown by Marion Butts and a 26-yard touchdown connection between Ferguson and Terry Anthony.

Win No. 173
Florida State 28, Florida 14
November 28, 1987
1987 Season: 10-1
Bowden, whose team went undefeated on the road in 1987, recorded his 100th victory at FSU in the win over Florida. The Gators took a 14-3 lead in the second quarter behind 2

Sammie Smith rushed for 116 yards against Florida in 1997.

touchdowns scored after an interception and blocked punt. Emmitt Smith had 2 short touchdown runs and 89 yards in the first half and appeared ready for an outstanding game. But the Seminoles dominated both sides of the ball in the second half as the offense scored 19 points while the McGowan-led defense held the Gators scoreless and Smith to 11 rushing yards. Bowden went to a ground game as the Seminoles held the ball for over 20 minutes and racked up 182 of their 279 rushing yards in the last two quarters. Sammie Smith finished the game with 116 rushing yards while Dexter Carter added another 111 yards.

Win No. 174 (Fiesta Bowl)
Florida State 31, Nebraska 28
January 1, 1988
1988 Season: 11-1
Third-ranked Nebraska held a 28-24 advantage and appeared to be headed for the game-clinching score with 6:58 remaining when Eric Hayes recovered a fumble that shifted the momentum in favor of the sixth-ranked Seminoles. The defensive tackle was one of several teammates who consistently and silently excelled throughout the year. The defenders even wrote the motto "Shut up and play football" on their wrist. After the recovery, the Seminoles took over at their 3-yard line and marched down the field. On fourth-and-goal from Nebraska's 15-yard line, Bowden had to decide whether to go for the touchdown or kick a field goal and then either recover an onside kick or hold the Cornhuskers and get the ball back. Ever the gambler, Bowden dove into his playbook for "460 Dip" and then put the hopes of the season on the arm of McManus. After Lewis and Pat Carter moved through their crossing pattern, Lewis broke into the clear and McManus hit him in the middle of

"As an accommodating, quotable, entertaining, affable, and consistent package, Bowden may have no equal," Hubert Mizell (St. Petersburg Times *sport columnist*) *once wrote. "His winning percentage is .999 among those approaching with a microphone, note pad, or camera."*

the end zone for the winning touchdown with 3:07 remaining. Nebraska almost pulled off the win when it moved the ball to the Florida State 2-yard line after a 56-yard pass completion. "I thought, that's it," Bowden told reporters after the game. "They've pulled this thing out." But Florida State held on for the win when officials nullified the pass play because of an illegal formation. McManus won the offensive MVP by completing 28-of-51 passes for 375 yards and 3 touchdowns. Gainer had 5 receptions for 89 yards and 2 touchdowns to end a stellar career. The Seminoles ended the season second in the final standings, their highest finish in school history. The win capped off a season that started what the NCAA would later call an official dynasty. As Bob Thomas of the *Jacksonville Times-Union* notes, the win "may have been the most significant victory in the Bobby Bowden era."

YEAR TWENTY–THREE: THE 1988 SEASON (11–1)

Win No. 175
Florida State 49, Southern Mississippi 13
September 10, 1988
1988 Season: 1-1
The Seminoles, who were slotted in the No. 1 position in three pre-season football rankings, were coming off a stunning 31-0 season-opening loss to Miami. Bowden, who had the luxury of a deep team and 13 returning starters, rallied the Seminoles to a win over the Golden Eagles, the first of 11 straight victories. The win over Southern Miss was established on the second play of the game when Deion Sanders intercepted a pass from Brett Favre and returned it 39 yards for a touchdown. Chip Ferguson led 3 first-half touchdown drives as the Seminoles built a 28-0 lead with four minutes remaining in the second quarter. Ferguson threw 3 touchdowns before Peter Tom Willis and Casey Weldon quarterbacked most of the second half. Dexter Carter and Lawrence Dawsey each scored 2 touchdowns.

Win No. 176
Florida State 24, Clemson 21
September 17, 1988
1988 Season: 2-1
Coach Bowden's most appropriate nickname is the "Riverboat Gambler." He has merited such a title through his inclination to call the riskiest and most unexpected play—with a playbook full of quick kicks, reverses, fake handoffs, flea-flickers, laterals, fake field goals, and any other chicanery possible—at the most unexpected time. One game best typifies his gambler approach. Actually, it was one play, which ESPN analyst Beano Cook called, "The greatest play since *My Fair Lady*." This most famous play and most courageous call—which Bowden called the "Puntrooskie" 30 years earlier when he first drew it up while coaching at South Georgia College—came on a rainy game in his first trip as the FSU coach to "Death Valley." The game was tied 21-21 with 1:30 remaining. Florida State had been unable to secure a first down and faced a fourth-and-four from its own 21-yard line. As FSU lined up in punt formation, it was obvious that the Seminoles would simply punt the ball and hope their defense could hold the Tigers. Bowden had other ideas, and he called for the

LeRoy Butler ran the "Puntrooskie" to perfection against Clemson in 1998.

ball to be snapped to up-back Dayne Williams, who gave the ball to junior reserve cornerback LeRoy Butler. As Williams and Alphonso Williams moved to the right along with the Clemson defense, Butler slipped to his left and ran 78 yards to the 1-yard line. Butler later explained to the media that he "had butterflies the size of pterodactyls" as the play unfolded. After Bowden let the clock wind down, Richie Andrews connected on a 19-yard field goal and Bowden had one of the gutsiest wins of his storied career. As Bob Thomas of the *Jacksonville Times-Union* would later write, "With one play, Florida State coach Bobby Bowden cemented his reputation as a gambler willing to risk everything for a victory." Lost in the "Puntrooskie" excitement was a key 76-yard punt return for a touchdown by Sanders that tied the game 14-14 in the third quarter. The punt return put Sanders in the spotlight as he informed the Clemson bench—similar to the "called shot" by Babe Ruth—before he went back to receive the punt that he would return the punt for a touchdown. He fulfilled his promise by returning the punt straight up the middle for a momentum-shifting score.

Win No. 177

Florida State 30, Michigan State 7

September 24, 1988

1988 Season: 3-1

Sanders and Butler completely shut down all passing lanes of the visiting Spartans. Sanders lived up to his "Prime Time" billing as the senior All American had a leaping goal-line interception at the end of the second quarter—in front of an ESPN national television audience—to preserve Florida State's 13-0 halftime lead. Butler did one better by returning his interception for a fourth-quarter touchdown. The two brilliant cornerbacks allowed only 1 pass completion on the day as the Spartans—the first Big Ten team to travel to Tallahassee—threw for only 25 yards. Kelvin Smith also made the highlights in the fourth quarter as he recovered a punt that had been blocked by Dedrick Dodge.

Win No. 178

Florida State 48, Tulane 28

October 1, 1988

1988 Season: 4-1

The Seminoles relied on the ground game as they threw 14 passes compared to 58 rushes against the Green Wave. Florida State ended the day with 434 rushing yards as Sammie Smith had the fourth-best yardage total in FSU history with 212 running yards. Seven other Seminoles combined to run for the remaining 222 yards. The Florida State defense forced 5 turnovers, led by a 34-yard interception return for a touchdown by Tracy Sanders for the first score of the game.

Win No. 179

Florida State 28, Georgia Southern 10

October 8, 1988

1988 Season: 5-1

An upset appeared likely as the visiting Eagles were leading 10-7 with under nine minutes remaining. But the Seminoles scored 3 touchdowns in the final eight minutes to pull out the come-from-behind victory in front of the homecoming fans. Ronald Lewis, who had 7 receptions for 140 yards, started the fourth-quarter scoring by catching a 16-yard touchdown pass from Ferguson. Dayne Williams and Chris Parker added 2 rushing touchdowns to complete the scoring.

Win No. 180

Florida State 45, East Carolina 21

October 15, 1988

1988 Season: 6-1

No Sammie Smith. No Dexter Carter. No Victor Floyd. No problem for the fourth-ranked Seminoles. As the only healthy running back, Parker got his first career start with a career game against the Pirates. After running for a touchdown and 59 yards in the first quarter, Parker ended the game with 158 yards and 2 touchdowns. Ferguson and Willis each threw touchdown passes while Marion Butts added a scoring run and Bill Mason had a field goal.

Win No. 181
Florida State 66, Louisiana Tech 3
October 22, 1988
1988 Season: 7-1
The Bulldogs had to be worried as Florida State's "close" win over East Carolina had dropped the Seminoles to No. 7 in the polls. Bowden, with 28 points in the first quarter alone, unleashed a prolific offense (346 yards passing and 185 yards rushing) and dominating defense. The FSU defense established the rout early when Howard Dinkins blocked a punt for a safety on the fourth play of the game. On the Bulldogs' next series, it was Stan Shiver's turn as he blocked a punt for a safety. Dedrick Dodge and Deion Sanders each had interceptions that they returned for touchdowns. On offense, four quarterbacks (Ferguson, Willis, Weldon, and Brad Johnson) each threw a touchdown pass.

Win No. 182
Florida State 59, South Carolina 0
November 5, 1988
1988 Season: 8-1
Ferguson, sidelined with an injury, was replaced by Willis, who went out and set a then school record for completion percentage. Against the Gamecocks, and in front of a national television audience, Willis was 17-of-20 for 271 yards and four touchdowns. The scoring began when Willis, starting the second game of his career, threw a 44-yard touchdown to Terry Anthony on FSU's second play. The Seminoles scored at least 14 points in every quarter with Willis hitting Dave Roberts for a second-quarter score and Dawsey for touchdowns on Florida State's first two possessions of the third quarter. Odell Haggins had 16 tackles to lead the FSU defense to its first shutout in two years.

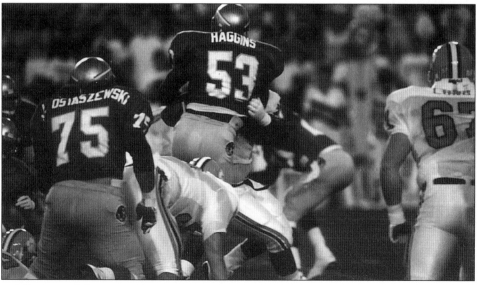

Odell Haggins led a strong FSU defense in 1988.

Win No. 183
Florida State 41, Virginia Tech 14
November 12, 1988
1988 Season: 9-1
Bowden has never lost to the Hokies in 14 career games. So this outcome was no surprise. The host Seminoles exploded for 34 unanswered points starting midway through the second quarter. Dayne Williams started the scoring streak with a 3-yard touchdown run. Butts had a 1-yard touchdown run and Ferguson and Willis each threw a scoring pass in the third quarter. Sammie Smith added his second touchdown run of the game with a 25-yard tackle-breaking score in the fourth quarter to end the scoring for the Seminoles.

Win No. 184
Florida State 52, Florida 17
November 26, 1988
1988 Season: 10-1
No FSU team scored more points against the Gators than the 1988 Seminoles. Led by Ferguson's 3 first-quarter touchdown passes, Florida State scored in every quarter and had 414 yards against a Florida defense that was ranked second in the nation. The ground game for both teams told the story. The FSU rushing offense, led by Sammie Smith's 109 yards, had 250 yards. Florida was held to 110 rushing yards, led by Emmitt Smith's 56 yards. The FSU defense, led by interceptions by John Hadley and Haggins, allowed 91 total yards in

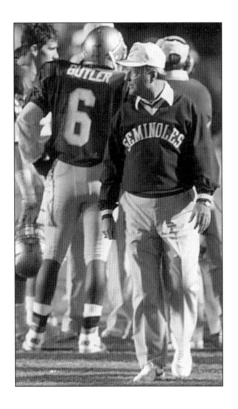

Bowden's offense scored often against Florida in 1988.

the first half and 73 passing yards for the game. Haggins, whose pick-off came after a deflection by linebacker Anthony Moss, ran 11 yards for a touchdown. A total of 21 FSU seniors left their last regular-season game at Doak Campbell with sweet memories in the blowout of the Gators.

Win No. 185 (Sugar Bowl)
Florida State 13, Auburn 7
January 2, 1989
1988 Season: 11-1
It had been 25 games since Auburn gave up 100 yards to a running back. Sammie Smith, who earned bowl MVP honors, played like his idol, Hershel Walker, as he ran for 115 yards against the No. 1 defense in the country. Auburn running backs struggled against the FSU defense: they lost 2 fumbles while running the ball 36 times for 108 yards. The Tiger passing attack was equally ineffective: Auburn threw for 162 yards and 3 interceptions in the loss. The last interception—by Deion Sanders in the end zone on the last play of the game—sealed the victory. The Florida State defense held strong when it needed to with a second-half shutout that allowed the Seminoles to escape victorious from New Orleans. With the win, Bowden had now led the Seminoles to seven straight bowls without a loss and back-to-back 11-win seasons. Florida State finished third in the polls behind Notre Dame and Miami.

Bowden laughs with freshman Charlie Ward before the 1989 season.

YEAR TWENTY-FOUR: THE 1989 SEASON (10–2)

Win No. 186

Florida State 31, Louisiana State 21

September 16, 1989

1989 Season: 1-2

The Seminoles started the year with two losses for the first time since Bowden's inaugural season in Tallahassee. While both losses were upsets by FSU opponents, the first was a complete shock, as Southern Mississippi's fourth-quarter drive beat the sixth-ranked Seminoles in Jacksonville. The second loss was at home to Clemson. On the road against LSU, Bowden's defense—led by All-America Odell Haggins, who had 10 tackles—shined with key fourth-quarter stops in front of an ESPN audience. Florida State, down 21-7 early in the fourth quarter, turned its season around under the direction of Peter Tom Willis. The fifth-year senior led two key comeback drives and had his first 300-yard passing effort. Willis would go on to lead the Seminoles to 10 straight victories and end the season breaking 14 school records.

Bowden congratulates Peter Tom Willis after a touchdown pass.

Win No. 187
Florida State 59, Tulane 9
September 23, 1989
1989 Season: 2-2
Willis threw for 2 touchdowns and 324 yards in the first-half as the Seminoles built a 31-0 lead. Casey Weldon, behind the protection of an offensive line that included future Tallahassee sports radio broadcaster Eric "Lulu" Luallen, replaced Willis and added 3 more passing touchdowns. His first pass was an 88-yard score to Amp Lee. LeRoy Butler had 2 interceptions while Terrell Buckley and Bryce Abbott each picked off a Green Wave pass. Lawrence Dawsey, who had at least 1 reception in every contest in 1989, ended the game with 3 receptions, including 2 touchdowns.

Win No. 188
Florida State 41, Syracuse 10
October 7, 1989
1989 Season: 3-2
In the Carrier Dome, the Florida State "Sack Pack" had 10 sacks to go along with 3 interceptions and 2 recovered fumbles. Butler picked off his fourth pass of the year and returned it 87 yards for a third-quarter score. Two plays earlier, Buckley scored the first touchdown of his career when he returned a punt 69 yards for a score after he fooled the Orangemen into thinking he had called for a fair catch. Florida State jumped out to a 17-3 halftime lead before adding 17 unanswered points in the third quarter and a touchdown run by Lee in the fourth. Shelton Thompson (2 sacks) and Kirk Carruthers (11 tackles and a sack) had big games to bolster a defense that allowed only 91 rushing yards. Carruthers ended the year with a team-leading 145 tackles.

Win No. 189
Florida State 41, Virginia Tech 7
October 14, 1989
1989 Season: 4-2
The "Sack Pack" put on another road show with 9 sacks at Lane Stadium. Thompson, Carruthers, and Eric Hayes each collected multiple sacks. The Florida State defense, while holding the Hokies to 45 rushing yards, intercepted 3 passes. Although the Virginia Tech defense came into the game ranked sixth in the country, the Seminoles found little resistance as they threw for 408 yards and rushed for another 126. Willis had his third 300-yard passing game of the season, throwing for 338 yards and 3 touchdowns.

Win No. 190
Florida State 22, Auburn 14
October 21, 1989
1989 Season: 5-2
With this win, Bowden secured his third straight victory over his former nemesis, including the Sugar Bowl victory 10 months earlier. Auburn scored 11 fourth-quarter points and was driving for what could have been a game-tying score in the final seconds. The Tigers

reached the FSU 18 yard line with only one play remaining. But the Florida State defense, which allowed a total of 92 rushing yards, blanketed the Auburn receivers to preserve the win. On offense, Edgar Bennett scored 2 short touchdowns and Lee led all rushers with 110 yards. A record-setting crowd attended the game in Tallahassee. Today, however, that attendance record doesn't rank among FSU's top-25 home crowds, as Bowden's dominating teams of the 1990s led to the expansion of Doak Campbell six times since the 1989 season.

Win No. 191
Florida State 24, Miami 10
October 28, 1989
1989 Season: 6-2
Back-to-back losses to the Hurricanes had kept the Seminoles from winning a national championship in both 1987 and 1988. Although FSU was out of the title hunt this season, a victory over Miami would get the team over a major stumbling block. Butler set the tone of the game when he intercepted a pass on the very first play from scrimmage. Florida State needed only one play to score when Dexter Carter ran for a 37-yard touchdown. With the score by Carter, who torched the No. 1–ranked Miami defense for 142 yards, the capacity home crowd was on its feet and remained there throughout the game. Carruthers led the defense with 2 interceptions, a key goal-line fumble recovery, and 16 tackles. The Florida State defense forced 6 Miami turnovers—including 3 second-quarter interceptions—and held the Hurricanes scoreless over the last three quarters.

Charlie Ward did it all for FSU, even punting 35 times as a freshman.

Win No. 192
Florida State 35, South Carolina 10
November 4, 1989
1989 Season: 7-2

The Seminoles gained an early 21-0 lead against their homecoming opponent. Willis began a three-game streak of 300-yard passing games by throwing for 362 yards and 3 touchdowns. While 11 different Seminoles caught passes, senior wide receivers led all receiving categories. Terry Anthony had 2 touchdown receptions and Bruce LaSane pulled in the third. Ronald Lewis led all receivers with 116 yards. Butler had his seventh interception of the season and Anthony Moss had 2 of the Florida State's 6 sacks.

Win No. 193
Florida State 57, Memphis State 20
November 18, 1989
1989 Season: 8-2

Willis had a career day, throwing for a personal-best 482 yards and a school-best 6 touchdowns against the Tigers. Even more amazing is that the FSU signal caller threw all his touchdowns in the first half, including 5 in the second quarter. Willis, and his third-quarter replacement, Brad Johnson, found 12 different receiving targets. Lewis led FSU with 2 touchdown receptions.

Win No. 194
Florida State 24, Florida 17
December 2, 1989
1989 Season: 9-2

Bowden won his third straight game over Florida. The in-state rivalry between the Seminoles and Gators became more intense during this contest, as both teams were called for multiple personal fouls. In the end, FSU was penalized for 134 yards while officials hit UF for 124 yards in penalties. Despite the bad blood between the two teams, Willis focused on the job at hand and established three FSU season passing records (total offense, pass completions, and passing yardage). He ended the game with 319 yards and 3 touchdowns. His first touchdown, a 62-yard strike to Anthony, put the Seminoles ahead 7-0 in the first quarter. Anthony ended the game with four receptions for 126 yards. A 24-yard field goal by Richie Andrews in the second quarter tied the game at 10. Florida State went up for good when Willis found LaSane for a 22-yard touchdown in the third quarter. A 6-yard touchdown pass in the fourth quarter from Willis to Dave Roberts finished the FSU scoring.

Win No. 195 (Fiesta Bowl)
Florida State 41, Nebraska 17
January 1, 1990
1989 Season: 10-2

After falling behind early in the first quarter, the Seminoles exploded for 34 unanswered points to secure the win. Four of the scores were touchdown passes from Willis, who went over the 300-yard mark for the seventh time on the season. He capped off a brilliant senior season with 5 touchdown passes and 422 yards. Anthony and Reggie Johnson each had 2 touchdown receptions. Anthony, Dawsey, and Lewis combined for 15 catches and 260 yards against the Cornhuskers. Florida State finished in the top three in the major polls. "I believe this team now could beat anybody," Bowden commented to reporters following the win. "We came back and peaked today. There's no question that, today, this team is the best in the country."

YEAR TWENTY-FIVE: THE 1990 SEASON (10–2)

Win No. 196
Florida State 45, East Carolina 24
September 8, 1990
1990 Season: 1-0
The third-ranked Seminoles looked to continue their winning ways as they had gone 32-4 over the previous three years. After suffering season-opening losses in back-to-back years, Florida State reversed that trend against the Pirates. Despite losing 14 starters from the previous season, Bowden had little trouble finding replacements. With first-round draft pick Dexter Carter gone to the NFL, Bowden now relied on Amp Lee at running back and

Peter Tom Willis won the Fiesta Bowl MVP Award to conclude the 1989 season.

Edgar Bennett at fullback. Against East Carolina, Lee led all rushers with 107 yards while Bennett scored 3 touchdowns. Terrell Buckley, coming off a splendid 1989 season and a spring practice in which he was named the top defensive player, had a 63-yard punt return for a touchdown and a 28-yard interception return that set up another score.

Win No. 197
Florida State 48, Georgia Southern 6
September 15, 1990
1990 Season: 2-0
During a 24-point fourth-quarter outburst, Buckley stole the show, returning a punt for a touchdown for the second consecutive game. Sean Jackson started the fourth-quarter rout with a 51-yard scamper, the longest run in two years for the Seminoles. Jackson, who preceded Warrick Dunn and Travis Minor as spectacular recruits from New Orleans, was a member of Bowden's heralded recruiting class of 1990, which included Clifton Abraham, Ken Alexander, William Floyd, Dan Footman, Corey Fuller, Lonnie Johnson, Marvin Jones, Kez McCorvey, Sam "Tiger" McMillon, Corey Sawyer, and Chris Weinke. Although Weinke's greatness wouldn't be seen until several years later, Jackson starred in just his second game by leading all rushers with 112 yards on 7 carries. On defense, Toddrick McIntosh recovered 1 fumble and forced another loose ball.

Win No. 198
Florida State 31, Tulane 13
September 22, 1990
1990 Season: 3-0
Of all the positions that were question marks going into the 1990 season, Bowden was most unsure about his quarterback situation. For the first time in three years, he had to rely on an underclassman to lead the offense. But Bowden, awarded an honorary doctorate earlier in the year by Samford University, overcame this handicap by eventually going back-and-forth with two juniors—and best friends—as starters. Waiting in the wings was sophomore Charlie Ward. Brad Johnson, whose performance in the spring earned him the starting nod over Casey Weldon to open the season, threw four touchdown passes in his first two career starts to open the season. Johnson, a pure drop-back passer who would go on to a great NFL career and lead the Tampa Bay Buccaneers to their first Super Bowl title in 2003, ran for a touchdown and combined with Weldon for 280 yards and 2 touchdowns against the Green Wave in the Superdome. Buckley continued his outstanding play by picking off his second pass of the season.

Win No. 199
Florida State 39, Virginia Tech 28
September 29, 1990
1990 Season: 4-0
This win against the visiting Hokies was one of the best come-from-behind victories for Bowden and FSU. Down 21-3 halfway into the second quarter, Bowden led a furious comeback as his Seminoles outscored Virginia Tech 36-7 over the rest of the contest. With

FSU trailing 28-25 near the end of third quarter, Buckley picked off a pass and returned it 53 yards for his third touchdown in four games. Late in the fourth quarter, the Seminoles secured the win when Kirk Carruthers and Marvin Jones forced a fumble that Errol McCorvey picked up and ran back 77 yards for a touchdown. Jones ended the year leading the Seminoles with 133 tackles. The win gave the Seminoles 14 consecutive victories, the longest winning streak in the nation.

Win No. 200
Florida State 42, Louisiana State 3
October 27, 1990
1990 Season: 5-2

After a tough loss to Miami and a last-second defeat at Auburn, the Seminoles took out their frustrations on LSU. The nationally televised win at Doak Campbell allowed Bowden—in his 15th year at FSU—to become the 11th Division I-A coach to pick up his 200th career win. Against the Tigers, the Florida State defense forced 5 turnovers and allowed only 66 yards passing and a first-quarter field goal. Weldon made his first career start and finished with 229 yards and 1 touchdown, while Lee had 3 short rushing scores in the first half.

The scoreboard honors Bowden on his 200th win.

Win No. 201
Florida State 41, South Carolina 10
November 3, 1990
1990 Season: 6-2
The defense was left particularly vulnerable at the beginning of the 1990 season, as the NFL drafted seven Seminoles from the 1989 squad and signed another four as free agents. Carruthers, one of only four returning starters on defense, led Bowden's young defenders to their second consecutive dominating game. On the road against the Gamecocks, the Seminoles had 2 interceptions, a blocked punt, and a season-high 7 sacks. The pickoffs by Buckley and Tommy Henry each led to touchdowns. The only touchdown surrendered by Florida State was in the fourth quarter when Bowden, who had received a death threat before the game, had his third-team unit on the field.

Win No. 202
Florida State 70, Cincinnati 21
November 10, 1990
1990 Season: 7-2
When FSU offensive coordinator Wayne McDuffie left before the 1990 season to take a

Lawrence Dawsey led a strong receiving unit in 1990.

position with the Atlanta Falcons, Bowden decided to turn his offense over to Brad Scott. The new coordinator had to work with a talented—but youthful—offense. Inexperience was evident at most positions, including the offensive line where guard Hayward Haynes was the only senior starter. The other starting linemen were Mike Morris, Reggie Dixon, Kevin Mancini, and Robbie Baker, who was replacing Outland Trophy finalist Michael Tanks. Despite the inexperience, Scott had his offense working to perfection as the Seminoles scored touchdowns on nine straight possessions against the Bearcats in this homecoming contest. Scott's offense was led by Weldon's 217 yards passing, Lawrence Dawsey's 141 receiving yards, and a 351-yard rushing attack in which 11 Seminoles touched the ball.

Win No. 203
Florida State 35, Memphis 3
November 17, 1990
1990 Season: 8-2
Dawsey, who had six 100-yard receiving games in 1990 and eight in his career, ended his senior campaign with four straight games over the century mark. One of his most memorable performances came against the Tigers in Orlando. The wide receiver, the only returning wideout from the "Fab Four" (Terry Anthony, Bruce LaSane, and Ronald Lewis), had 3 carries for 67 yards and 8 receptions for 133 yards. Two of his catches were for touchdowns of 45 and 17 yards. Over the course of his career, he caught a pass in 31

The "Fab Four" was (left to right) Ronald Lewis, Terry Anthony, Lawrence Dawsey, and Bruce LaSane.

consecutive games, breaking the national record held by Ron Sellers. Most of his rushing yards came on a 63-yard reverse. Carruthers had a fumble recovery and McCorvey added an interception while Weldon threw 3 touchdowns in the win.

Win No. 204
Florida State 45, Florida 30
December 1, 1990
1990 Season: 9-2
The game was the first battle between Bowden and Steve Spurrier as the in-state rivalry took on a whole new dimension. The two head coaches butted heads on and off the field. "Steve had a way of stimulating [the series], irritating it, riling you up," said Bowden years later. "Most coaches work differently than that." Spurrier's strategy had admirers and detractors. As renown sports historian Richard Crepeau once noted, "Spurrier is one of the best known and the most loved and hated figures in the State of Florida, a genius or an evil genius." While the new Florida coach added intensity to the already hostile FSU/UF rivalry, he struggled to beat Bowden before he exited the college football scene after the 2001 season. Bowden, who held an 8-5-1 record against Spurrier, noted after the coach's departure to the NFL, "Am I going to miss him? In a little way." Although Spurrier was new on the scene at Florida in 1990, the outcome of the game was not new, as Bowden's eighth-ranked Seminoles won their fourth consecutive game over the sixth-ranked Gators. Weldon, Dawsey, and Lee led the offensive assault for FSU. Weldon had 325 yards passing

Casey Weldon led FSU to six straight wins to end the 1990 season.

while Lee had 147 yards rushing. Dawsey, who caught a 76-yard touchdown from Weldon on the second play of the game, had 172 receiving yards in the win. The Florida State defense forced a fumble on Florida's first play, which resulted in a 47-yard field goal by Richie Andrews to put the Seminoles ahead 10-0. After a UF field goal, Weldon hit Lee for an 8-yard touchdown and a 17-3 first-quarter lead. Four rushing touchdowns, 2 each by Lee and Bennett, capped FSU's scoring and secured the win in front of a record-setting crowd at Doak Campbell.

Win No. 205 (Blockbuster Bowl)
Florida State 24, Penn State 17
December 28, 1990
1990 Season: 10-2
Going into the game at Joe Robbie Stadium, Bowden had firmly established himself in second place on the list of most victories by active coaches. Joe Paterno was the man in front of Bowden. The two legends squared off for the only time in their careers in the inaugural Blockbuster Bowl. The only other time that two 200-game winners had coached against each other was in 1978, when Bear Bryant met Woody Hayes. Against the seventh-ranked Nittany Lions, the sixth-ranked Seminoles were led by Weldon's 248 passing yards, Dawsey's 107 receiving yards, and Lee's 86 rushing yards. Lee took home the MVP award, as he had 2 touchdown runs in the first half. But it was the defense that secured the win. Over the final six minutes of the game, after the Nittany Lions had pulled to within seven points, the FSU defense stepped up in back-to-back series. The first defensive stand resulted

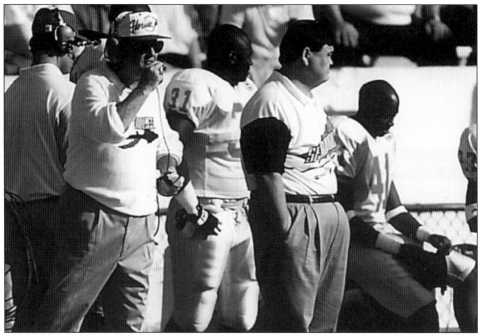

Chaplin Clint Purvis (right) is a valuable member of the FSU family.

in a punt. The second and final stand of the game came when John Davis intercepted a pass that allowed the Seminoles to run out the clock. The Seminoles ended the year ranked fourth in the country.

YEAR TWENTY-SIX: THE 1991 SEASON (11-2)

Win No. 206
Florida State 44, Brigham Young 28
August 28, 1991
1991 Season: 1-0
Pre-season prognosticators considered the Seminoles a national championship favorite as FSU started the season a unanimous No. 1. Florida State went to Anaheim to play the Cougars in the second annual Disneyland/Pigskin Classic. "If you're ever going to play in one of these preseason games," Bowden commented, "you want to do it when you've got some experienced players returning." FSU picked the perfect time as 67 of Bowden's 79 lettermen were returning, including 8 starters on offense and 9 on defense. For BYU, Heisman Trophy winner Ty Detmer led the offense. But it was Casey Weldon who stole the show and won the game MVP. The eventual winner of the Johnny Unitas Golden Arm Award threw for 268 yards and 2 touchdowns against the Cougars. Edgar Bennett led all scorers by rushing for 2 touchdowns and catching a pass for another.

Win No. 207
Florida State 38, Tulane 11
September 7, 1991
1991 Season: 2-0
For the first time in FSU history, the Seminoles played in front of a home crowd as the No. 1 team in the nation. Bowden's squad didn't disappoint, as only 10 seconds into FSU's first drive, Weldon found Lonnie Johnson for a 78-yard touchdown. The tight ends caught all four of Weldon's touchdowns. Beginning with the game against the Green Wave, Bowden's game plans involved his tight ends more frequently in 1991 than he did in the past or would do in the future. Johnson ended the game with 6 receptions for 154 yards while Warren Hart had another 3 catches that all resulted in short touchdowns.

Win No. 208
Florida State 58, Western Michigan 0
September 14, 1991
1991 Season: 3-0
With the shutout at Doak Campbell, Bowden moved ahead of former Clemson and Rice coaching legend Jess Neely into seventh place on the all-time wins list. The blowout allowed Bowden a chance to showcase some of his future talent as eight different Seminoles scored. Florida State had a complete returning backfield with Bennett and Amp Lee. While Lee had 8 carries against the Broncos, William Floyd and Tiger McMillon both had second-quarter touchdown runs. Floyd, who had 5 touchdowns on the season, provided Bowden with a strong one-two punch at fullback behind Bennett.

Win No. 209
Florida State 51, Michigan 31
September 28, 1991
1991 Season: 4-0
This victory ranks high on Bowden's list of most memorable games. That's because his chicanery led the No. 1 Seminoles, playing against the No. 3 Wolverines in front of 106,145 spectators, to their first victory in Ann Arbor. Two trick plays on one first-quarter drive gave the Seminoles the lead for good. Bowden first called for a lateral from Weldon to Charlie Ward, who ran to the other side of the field. Ward then found Weldon for a 29-yard completion that led to what appeared to be a short field goal attempt. But instead of placing the ball down for the kick, holder and backup quarterback Brad Johnson picked it up and shoveled the ball to Floyd for a 4-yard touchdown pass and a 13-7 lead. Weldon finished the day with 268 yards and 3 touchdowns. The FSU defense had 3 sacks and 3 interceptions while scoring 2 touchdowns. One defensive score came on the first play of the game when Terrell Buckley picked off a pass and took it back 40 yards for a touchdown. The cornerback, who would win the Jim Thorpe Award for his performance in 1991, would forego his senior season for the NFL after leading the nation with 12 interceptions. Kirk Carruthers, who finished the season second on the team with 7 sacks, returned to his home state and had 19 tackles in the win.

Win No. 210
Florida State 46, Syracuse 14
October 5, 1991
1991 Season: 5-0
The visiting Orangemen, undefeated and ranked 10th in the country, couldn't contain Florida State's explosive offense. The Seminoles, while falling behind 14-7, stormed back to score 39 unanswered points over the final three quarters. Weldon, who finished his career at FSU with a 17-2 record as the starting quarterback, led the offensive assault, passing for 347 yards and 3 touchdowns. The FSU defense held Syracuse scoreless over the final three quarters with the help of interceptions by Buckley and Clifton Abraham.

Win No. 211
Florida State 33, Virginia Tech 20
October 12, 1991
1991 Season: 6-0
After the win in Orlando, Florida State improved to 2-0 on the season in neutral site games. FSU was victorious by applying defensive pressure and forcing four Hokie turnovers. Leon Fowler picked off the first of 3 FSU interceptions. His first-quarter interception set up Bennett's 8-yard touchdown that tied the game 7-7. Fowler ended the season leading the FSU secondary with 59 tackles. Buckley, intercepting a pass for the third consecutive game, ran back his second-quarter pickoff 71 yards for a touchdown that put Florida State ahead 14-7. He added another interception in the fourth quarter to preserve the win. Carruthers had 15 tackles and Marvin Jones added another 13 stops to lead the defense.

Terrell Buckley intercepted a pass in three straight games during the 1991 season.

Win No. 212
Florida State 39, Middle Tennessee State 10
October 19, 1991
1991 Season: 7-0
The Florida State defense recovered 2 fumbles, blocked a punt, and recorded its third safety of the year in the homecoming win. Carl Simpson, who had one of 8 total sacks against the Blue Raiders, ended the season with the most sacks (11) in school history. On offense, the Seminoles scored a touchdown in every quarter beginning with their first possession when Weldon hit Shannon Baker with a 5-yard touchdown pass. Baker, who ended the year with a team-leading 30 receptions for 451 yards and four touchdowns, had 6 receptions for 100 yards and 2 touchdowns.

Win No. 213
Florida State 27, Louisiana State 16
October 26, 1991
1991 Season: 8-0
In a preseason publication, ESPN's Tim Brando had selected Bowden as the nation's best coach. Brando emphasized Bowden's dominance over SEC opponents by stating that "Pound for pound he is the best. What he's accomplished against the Southeastern Conference is amazing. He nails them." In a downpour at Tiger Stadium, Bowden allowed the legs of Lee and the dominance of his defense to do the hammering. While the Seminoles ran up 212 rushing yards on the night, the Tigers were held to 27 rushing yards

127

on 27 carries. Florida State, down 16-7 at halftime, stormed back with the first of 3 unanswered touchdowns on a 22-yard scoring connection from Weldon to Lee. FSU then added two 1-yard touchdown runs—one each by Lee and Floyd—to finish off the come-from-behind effort. Lee's final touchdown was set up by a fumble forced by Toddrick McIntosh and recovered by Carruthers. Lee, who had his first of 3 touchdowns in the second quarter, had his last 100-yard game for FSU when he carried the ball 24 times for 112 yards against the Tigers.

Win No. 214
Florida State 40, Louisville 15
November 2, 1991
1991 Season: 9-0
As the FSU season progressed, the defense got better, ending the year ranked among the top five in the nation. Against the Cardinals, FSU forced 7 turnovers and held Louisville to 35 rushing yards. Six of the takeaways were through interceptions, which set a school record. On the year, the Seminoles had a total of 25 interceptions, led by Buckley's 12. At Louisville, Florida State was led by Buckley's 2 pickoffs in the freezing and windy weather. Jones, who had 10 tackles, intercepted a pass to set up FSU's first score. The sophomore inside linebacker—who again led the Seminoles in tackles with 125—became the youngest finalist for the Lombardi Award. On offense, a knee injury forced Weldon to the sideline, and Brad Johnson filled in as a most capable replacement.

Win No. 215
Florida State 38, South Carolina 10
November 9, 1991
1991 Season: 10-0
Weldon returned from his injury and threw touchdown passes to Baker, Lee, and Floyd as the Seminoles—No. 1 for the 12th consecutive week—took a commanding 17-0 lead. Lee and Sean Jackson each had a 1-yard touchdown run in the third quarter to seal the win. The Florida State defense held the Gamecocks to 92 yards rushing while Buckley picked up his school-record ninth interception of the season. The win gave Florida State its longest winning streak in school history at 16 games. Also, with five consecutive 10-win seasons, Bowden joined Bear Bryant and Bud Wilkinson as the only coaches to accomplish that feat.

Win No. 216 (Cotton Bowl)
Florida State 10, Texas A&M 2
January 1, 1992
1992 Season: 11-2
The regular season had ended with heart-wrenching losses. The first loss came at the hands of the Hurricanes, who won the game 17-16 in the first "Wide Right" contest. The second defeat was to the Gators, who were able to hold on to a 14-9 victory in a defensive battle. In the Cotton Bowl, the fifth-ranked Seminoles faced the ninth-ranked Aggies for the first time since 1968. Texas A&M came into the bowl with a nine-game winning streak after going undefeated in the Southwest Conference. The bright spot on offense was Sean

Bowden accepts the Cotton Bowl trophy after defeating Texas A&M.

Jackson, who made his first career start and came away with 112 yards and the offensive MVP award. The only touchdown scored was a 4-yard run by Weldon in the first quarter. Gerry Thomas added a fourth-quarter 27-yard field goal to end the scoring. Texas A&M, whose only score was a Quentin Coryatt sack of Weldon for a safety in the first quarter, couldn't move the ball against the FSU defense. The Seminoles secured the win when they shut out the Texas A&M offense and held the Aggies to 57 rushing yards and 123 passing yards while forcing 8 turnovers. Bowden, by leaving his 10th consecutive bowl game without a loss, improved to 11-3-1 in bowl games. The Seminoles, who ended the season at No. 4, had now tied an NCAA record by winning their seventh straight bowl game.

YEAR TWENTY-SEVEN: THE 1992 SEASON (11-1)

Win No. 217
Florida State 48, Duke 21
September 5, 1992
1992 Season: 1-0
The Seminoles joined the Atlantic Coast Conference (ACC) in 1991 but didn't compete as full-fledged members until the 1992 season. The multi-talented Charlie Ward, who beat out Kenny Felder in spring practice for the starting nod, made the first start of his career against the visiting Blue Devils. Ward had much more collegiate experience on the basketball court than the football field and entered the season having completed only 5 passes at Florida State. In basketball, he was coming off a splendid season at point guard, where he led FSU to its first "Sweet Sixteen" in 20 years. He then settled in as quarterback against Duke and passed for 269 yards and four touchdowns. He also ran for a 6-yard score. Ward, who would end his career with 19 Florida State passing and total offense records along with a Heisman Trophy and national championship, eventually became the most decorated player in the history of college football. In 2003, he was honored as one of the top three male athletes in the history of the ACC, with Michael Jordan and David Thompson leading the list.

Charlie Ward led FSU to 11 wins in 1992.

Win No. 218

Florida State 24, Clemson 20

September 12, 1992

1992 Season: 2-0

Charlie Ward again showed flashes of greatness—including a dramatic fourth-quarter comeback—as he threw for 259 yards and 2 touchdowns on the road before spectators in "Death Valley" and on ESPN. William Floyd started the scoring with a 1-yard touchdown run at the end of the first quarter. Tommy Henry's interception then set up a 29-yard field goal by Dan Mowrey. The Tigers responded with 13 straight points to take a 13-10 lead in the third quarter. But Clifton Abraham's 51-yard fumble return set up an 11-yard touchdown pass from Ward to Matt Frier. Early in the fourth quarter, however, Clemson responded to take a 20-17 lead. Ward again showed his brilliance by directing a time-consuming 77-yard drive with less than six minutes remaining. He finished the drive with a 9-yard touchdown pass to Kevin Knox to pull out the victory.

Win No. 219

Florida State 34, North Carolina State 13

September 19, 1992

1992 Season: 3-0

While Ward was still settling into Bowden's offense, the Florida State defense kept the Seminoles winning. Coming into the season, Bowden knew he needed to find replacements at cornerback, as both starters were gone, including Jim Thorpe Award winner Terrell Buckley. In stepped Henry, Abraham, Corey Sawyer, and Corey Fuller. Against the Wolfpack in North Carolina, it was Sawyer who stole the show by tying a school record with 3 interceptions. FSU got on the scoreboard when—after Sawyer's first interception—Ward connected with Tamarick Vanover for a 60-yard touchdown. Ward threw for 2 more scores with completions of 32 and 44 yards to Shannon Baker.

Win No. 220

Florida State 35, Wake Forest 7

September 26, 1992

1992 Season: 4-0

The Seminoles had four returning lettermen at wide receiver in 1992, led by Baker. However, against the visiting Demon Deacons, it was Vanover's time to shine. The freshman scored on a 96-yard kickoff return and an 18-yard reception in the win. Sawyer set up Vanover's touchdown catch when the cornerback eluded several defenders on an impressive 36-yard punt return. Floyd and Tiger McMillon each scored on short touchdown runs in the second quarter as the Seminoles built a 28-7 halftime lead. Sean Jackson provided late-game highlights, beating the defense around the corner for an 88-yard score. The Seminoles next traveled to Miami where they suffered their only loss of the season in the second "Wide Right" game. The loss to the Hurricanes—while a major setback—changed Bowden's offensive strategy. Bowden had put a shotgun offense (an offense that originated in the NFL in 1960) into the playbook during the off season for two-minute situations. Against Miami, Ward went into the shotgun at the end of each half, and moved

Tiger McMillon carried the rushing load against Wake Forest.

the Seminoles down the field with relative ease. At the time, Bowden noted that he thought FSU should be in that formation all the time. However, it took him two more weeks—during a 22-point fourth-quarter rally against Georgia Tech—before he was convinced to permanently switch to that offense. After the game against the Yellow Jackets, FSU went to the shotgun formation on a permanent basis.

Win No. 221
Florida State 36, North Carolina 13
October 10, 1992
1992 Season: 5-1
Although deflated after the setback at Miami, the Seminoles returned to Tallahassee and methodically outscored the Tar Heels. After a 1-yard touchdown run by Jackson, Sawyer returned a punt 74 yards for a touchdown as FSU built a 13-0 first-quarter lead. Florida State then added a field goal by Mowrey. A tailback pass set up the next score as Ward handed to Jackson, who stopped and hit Vanover for a 46-yard gain. Floyd then ran for a 1-yard touchdown. Ken Alexander later recovered a fumble, setting up a quarterback keeper by Ward from the 3-yard line. Vanover electrified the crowd when he took a reverse from the 5-yard line to end the scoring.

Win No. 222

Florida State 29, Georgia Tech 24

October 17, 1992

1992 Season: 6-1

Florida State trailed the Yellow Jackets 21-7 at the start of the fourth quarter. With a two-touchdown deficit, Bowden went to a fast-break, no-huddle offense. Ward—working from the shotgun—amazed the fans in Atlanta by collecting 206 of the 207 yards FSU accumulated on three fourth-quarter touchdown drives. On Florida State's first offensive possession in the final stanza, Ward began the comeback by completing 6 passes and scrambling for an amazing 24-yard run on a broken play to set up a 1-yard touchdown run by Floyd. After a Georgia Tech field goal, Ward led the Seminoles on an 80-yard drive that ended with his 5-yard quarterback keeper to pull the Seminoles to within four points with just over three minutes remaining. After Sawyer recovered Mowrey's on-side kick, Ward—faced with a fourth-and-five—threaded a 17-yard touchdown pass to Kez McCorvey for the go-ahead score. A safety by Reggie Freeman with under a minute remaining assured the FSU victory. Star "bandit" outside linebacker Derrick Brooks had a season-high 18 tackles in the win. Florida State's 22-point rally changed the course of the FSU offense, as Bowden decided to stick with the shotgun formation after Ward's tremendous success against the Yellow Jackets.

William Floyd scores a touchdown against Georgia Tech in 1992.

Win No. 223

Florida State 13, Virginia 3

October 31, 1992

1992 Season: 7-1

Bowden picked up his 150th Florida State victory—and matched the win total of all seven FSU coaches who preceded him—on a rainy and cold Halloween night at Scott Stadium. "It's ironic my 150th victory at Florida State would also be the 300th in the school's history," Bowden said after the season. The game featured another comeback as FSU scored 2 touchdowns after the Cavaliers scored first in the second quarter. The first Seminole score—a 27-yard touchdown pass from Ward to Vanover—put FSU up 7-3 at halftime. Ward then ended a long drive near the end of the third quarter with a 16-yard touchdown run. Despite the absence of the injured Jones, the Florida State defense held strong in the fourth quarter as Brooks (10 tackles and 1 1/2 sacks) and his teammates, who had 3 takeaways in the game, held the Cavaliers to 195 yards of total offense. Robert Stevenson led the offensive line that opened holes for McMillon and his 138 yards rushing, the most yards for an FSU rusher in 1992.

Win No. 224

Florida State 69, Maryland 21

November 7, 1992

1992 Season: 8-1

Florida State won the conference title as the Seminoles went through their first ACC schedule without a blemish after crushing Maryland in front of a record-setting crowd (64,127) during homecoming at Doak Campbell. The offense worked Bowden's Fast Break system to perfection against the Terrapins as Ward ran his shotgun operation for a score on each offensive series in the first half. Kevin Knox scored twice before halftime while Ward, Floyd, McCorvey, and Clyde Allen each added first-half touchdowns. Bowden's "Crocodile Play" set up Allen's score as Ward threw to Baker, who then returned a pass to Ward for a 28-yard gain. Ward ran for 111 yards and threw for 395 yards. The Seminoles broke 11 FSU records, including 858 yards of total offense and 10 touchdowns.

Win No. 225

Florida State 70, Tulane 7

November 14, 1992

1992 Season: 9-1

The Seminoles unveiled shiny garnet pants for this game. With Walter Payton on the sidelines, Florida State put on a sweet offensive show with 35 points in the first quarter and 49 unanswered points to begin the game. Ward's no-huddle offense continued to roll with 488 total yards in the win. In the first quarter alone, Ward threw touchdown passes to Baker, McMillon, and McCorvey. He added a fourth touchdown when he hit Allen in the second quarter. Carl Simpson had 2 sacks and FSU picked off four Green Wave passes. In a game with many stars, Baker and Abraham stood out. Baker took a reverse from Vanover and returned a kickoff 90 yards for a score while Abraham returned a punt 18 yards for a score and returned an interception 32 yards for another touchdown.

Bowden called all the right plays against Tulane.

Win No. 226
Florida State 45, Florida 24
November 28, 1992
1992 Season: 10-1

Before the 1992 season, Bowden looked at the schedule and told reporters, "Gosh am I glad we don't have to play Miami and Florida back-to-back." The break between the two contests proved just what Bowden needed as Florida State had no problem with the Gators in front of yet another record-setting crowd (68,311) at Doak Campbell. Ward threw for 331 yards in the game. Fuller set the stage for FSU's win with an interception on Florida's first possession. Jackson then carried what Bowden called "the entire Florida roster" for the first score, a 10-yard touchdown run. Vanover made sure FSU always had good field position, as he had several long returns, including a 52-yard return after faking the reverse and a 76-yard return in which he eluded six defenders. With the win, Bowden established the Seminoles as a true college football dynasty, as Florida State became the first school with six straight seasons of at least 10 wins.

Win No. 227 (Orange Bowl)
Florida State 27, Nebraska 14
January 1, 1993
1992 Season: 11-1

Using its shotgun offense to build a large lead before heavy rain turned the game into a defensive battle, Florida State became the first team in history to win eight straight bowl appearances. With Bowden and Tom Osborne (195 wins) squaring off, this was a battle between two coaches who ranked second and third on the list of most victories by active coaches. Bowden improved to 5-2 against the Cornhuskers as the early momentum favored the Seminoles. Jones, who had 14 tackles, including 1 sack, led the defense on a key fourth-and-one stop in the first quarter. Ward, who won his first of two bowl MVP awards, then took over and directed his shotgun offense on a drive that ended with a 25-yard touchdown to Vanover. After a 29-yard reverse by Vanover and a 28-yard connection from Ward to Jackson, Mowrey added a 40-yard field goal to put the Seminoles ahead 10-0. Dan Footman's recovery of a fumble inside the 5-yard line gave Ward another opportunity, and he capitalized with a 4-yard touchdown pass to McCorvey for a 17-point lead. Mowrey then kicked a 24-yard field goal to give FSU a 20-0 lead. After Nebraska finally broke the shutout near the end of the first half, the teams traded scores in the second half as the rain slowed both offenses. The FSU defense held the potent Cornhuskers to 290 yards of total offense. In addition to Jones, other Seminoles with sacks were Simpson, Footman, Freeman, and Lavon Brown. Florida State ended the year ranked second in the nation.

Orange Bowl MVP Charlie Ward electrified Seminole fans the entire season.

YEAR TWENTY-EIGHT: THE 1993 SEASON (12-1)

Win No. 228
Florida State 42, Kansas 0
August 28, 1993
1993 Season: 1-0
Florida State Sports Information Director Wayne Hogan noted before the season that "Sure, Bobby Bowden craves a national championship. There is a good chance he'll win one along the way." Bowden, who made history as one-half of the first father-son pair to coach a major program when his son Terry took over at Auburn in 1993, would not have to wait long, as his top-ranked Seminoles began their title hunt at Meadowlands Stadium in the 11th Annual Kickoff Classic. Charlie Ward had his fast-break offense primed to go, while Derrick Brooks began his junior year with a dominating performance on a hot day in New Jersey. But it was the collective effort of the defense that everyone was talking about. Bowden knew his defense would be special, as Brooks (13 tackles) and his teammates made a historic stop of the Jayhawks on a 12-play, goal-line stand in the second quarter. Kansas, down 14-0 but poised to score from the 1-yard-line, hit a stone wall. The Seminoles stopped Kansas six times inside the 1-yard line to preserve the shutout. After the final stop by Corey Sawyer and Ken Alexander, Florida State went 99 yards for its third touchdown. Four Seminoles combined to throw for 290 yards, with game MVP Kez McCorvey catching 5 passes for 107 yards.

Win No. 229
Florida State 45, Duke 7
September 4, 1993
1993 Season: 2-0
The rain didn't affect Ward. In just over two quarters of action, the signal caller threw 2 touchdowns and ran for a third score. Florida State, which had 628 yards of total offense, faced little resistance on the road against the Blue Devils. Scott Bentley had 2 field goals, while Sean Jackson ran for a 54-yard touchdown and Pooh Bear Williams added another 47-yard score. The Seminoles had 279 rushing yards with Jackson leading all rushers with 107 yards. The FSU defense allowed only 17 yards rushing while forcing four turnovers. Brooks started a 22-point second quarter by returning an interception 32 yards for a touchdown.

Win No. 230
Florida State 57, Clemson 0
September 11, 1993
1993 Season: 3-0
The Tigers, ranked 17th in the country, suffered their worst loss in six decades in front of a record-setting crowd at the newly expanded Doak Campbell. Florida State scored at least 10 points in every quarter, while the defense pitched its second shutout in three games. In just three quarters of work, Ward completed 25-of-33 passes for 317 yards and 4 touchdowns. Danny Kanell and the entire second team offense entered the game for one

play in the second quarter. The scheme, known as Bowden's Kentucky Derby Offense, worked to perfection as Kanell hit Lonnie Johnson for a 78-yard touchdown. Johnson had 2 receptions in the game, both for touchdowns. The FSU defense scored twice with Brooks involved on both plays. In the first score, Brooks blocked a second-quarter punt that Clifton Abraham recovered in the end zone. The second score came when Brooks returned his fumble recovery 83 yards for a touchdown. Abraham had an outstanding game with a goal line stop and an interception in the end zone to preserve the shutout.

Win No. 231
Florida State 33, North Carolina 7
September 18, 1993
1993 Season: 4-0
The Seminoles traveled to Chapel Hill to face the 13th-ranked team in the country. North Carolina jumped out to a 7-0 lead before Florida State scored 33 unanswered points. While Ward worked his quick-strike offense for 303 yards and 2 touchdowns, it was the FSU defense that led Bowden to victory by forcing 3 turnovers. The final turnover of the game came when Brooks scored in his third straight game by intercepting a pass and returning it 49 yards for a touchdown.

Win No. 232
Florida State 51, Georgia Tech 0
October 2, 1993
1993 Season: 5-0
Ward, who threw four touchdowns, led an FSU offense that racked up 582 yards. The Seminoles didn't score in the first 21 minutes until a short field goal by Bentley. Ward then threw touchdown passes to Johnson and Kez McCorvey to give the Seminoles a 16-0 halftime lead. Ward's roommate, Warrick Dunn, who ended his freshman year with 10 touchdowns, then took over as he found the end zone for 3 touchdowns. The FSU defense dominated again with its third shutout of the season by holding the Yellow Jackets to 45 passing yards and 65 rushing yards. Derrick Alexander had 10 tackles, including 2 sacks. Although the Seminoles had outscored their opponents 228-14 in their first five games of the season, it was their opponent in week six that would determine the outcome of the season.

Win No. 233
Florida State 28, Miami 10
October 9, 1993
1993 Season: 6-0
Bowden had lost three straight games to the third-ranked Hurricanes. Each of those losses knocked the Seminoles out of contention for the national championship. But this season, the FSU offense, which had 450 yards in the win, scored 3 early touchdowns to ensure that the game would not come down to a last-minute, field goal attempt. Jackson ran for a 69-yard touchdown to begin the scoring in front of a record-setting crowd at Doak Campbell. After the Hurricanes got on the board, Ward responded with a 72-yard touchdown pass to

Bowden discusses the game with Miami Coach Dennis Erickson (left).

Matt Frier. Ward then added a 2-yard touchdown run early in the second quarter. Strong safety Devin Bush preserved the win by returning his first career interception in the fourth quarter for a 40-yard touchdown.

Win No. 234
Florida State 40, Virginia 14
October 16, 1993
1993 Season: 7-0
The 15th-ranked Cavaliers came into Doak Campbell undefeated and poised for an upset in the game televised on ESPN. But the Seminoles jumped out to a 30-0 halftime lead, beginning with Tamarick Vanover's 86-yard touchdown reception from Ward early in the first quarter. Ward ended the game with 3 touchdown passes and an 18-yard touchdown run. Florida State rolled up 560 yards of total offense, including Ward's 322 passing yards.

Win No. 235
Florida State 54, Wake Forest 0
October 30, 1993
1993 Season: 8-0
Bowden, who relied on a key reserve and dominant defense to pick up the win and his fourth shutout on the season, moved past Michigan's Bo Schembechler into sixth place for all-time coaching victories. Ward suffered a bruised cartilage injury in the second quarter and was unable to return. Jon Stark led the Seminoles to 3 second-half scores and the

victory. The offense continued to roll as Florida State had 414 rushing yards and 233 passing yards. Dunn carried the Seminoles to their 18th consecutive homecoming win with 162 rushing yards and 2 touchdowns on only 8 carries. Jackson added another 116 yards on the ground. The FSU defense had 5 sacks and scored a touchdown when Abraham returned an interception 29 yards for a touchdown.

Win No. 236
Florida State 49, Maryland 20
November 6, 1993
1993 Season: 9-0

With Ward injured and on the sideline, Danny Kanell stepped in for his first career start and completed 28-of-38 passes for 341 yards and 5 touchdowns. Florida State, which had 526 yards of offense in the game and built a 14-0 second-quarter lead, scored its first four touchdowns through the air. Kanell, whose first touchdown came on a 17-yard strike to McCorvey, also had touchdown passes to Frier, Jackson, and Kevin Knox. McCorvey ended the game with 10 receptions for 122 yards. The Seminoles ended the scoring on 2 rushing scores with Vanover's 6-yard run and Jackson's 19-yard scamper. The win at Byrd Stadium gave FSU its 16th consecutive victory and its second consecutive conference championship.

Win No. 237
Florida State 62, North Carolina State 3
November 20, 1993
1993 Season: 10-1

The visiting Wolfpack knew they were in trouble. The Seminoles were coming off their only loss of the season, a heartbreaker against the Irish in Notre Dame Stadium—the toughest stadium, according to Bowden, in which he ever coached. Florida State, still clinging to their national championship aspirations, took out their frustrations on the Wolfpack. FSU forced 6 turnovers and jumped out to a 14-0 lead only five minutes into the game when the Seminoles recovered 2 North Carolina State fumbles after only three Wolfpack offensive plays. Ward, who in the game broke the school career record for total offense, led a group of five seniors who scored in their final home game. Knox, Frier, Johnson, and Clyde Allen all found the end zone. Sawyer led the defense with 2 interceptions and a fumble recovery.

Win No. 238
Florida State 33, Florida 21
November 27, 1993
1993 Season: 11-1

Charlie Ward secured his legendary status by throwing for what was then an FSU record 38-of-53 passes for 446 yards and four touchdowns. It was his final touchdown pass that cemented the win after the Gators had pulled to within six points at 27-21. The game-ending score came when Ward was forced to scramble to his left, where he saw Dunn down the sideline. Dunn caught the pass and, with an impressive block from Vanover, raced 79 yards for the score. Dunn ended the game with 140 receiving yards and 33 rushing yards. The win at the Swamp locked up the Heisman Trophy for Ward, as the All American had 475 yards of total offense. The Florida State defense was also spectacular with 6 sacks while setting an FSU record by holding the Gators to minus-33 yards on the ground. The victory, in front of a then state-record 85,507 fans, allowed the Seminoles back into the national championship picture. Two days after the regular-season finale, Sandy D'Alemberte was appointed president of FSU. D'Alemberte, who led the university to unprecedented academic, structural, architectural, and fiscal growth during his nearly decade-long leadership, was instrumental in leading the athletics renewal at Florida State. One of his key successes was bringing in Athletics Director Dave Hart 15 months after taking over the presidency. Under Hart's leadership, the FSU Athletics Department developed into one the top programs in the nation. While a strong talent base of athletics officials (including Andy Urbanic, Rob Wilson, Bernie Waxman, Randy Oravetz, and Greg Phillips) was in place when he arrived, Hart has surrounded himself with a strong cast of leaders over the past eight years. Among some of his talented hires who work closest with Bowden and the FSU football program are Bob Minnix, Pam Overton, and Jon Jost.

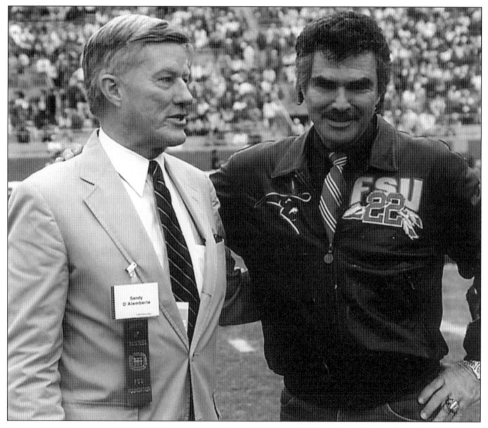

Sandy D'Alemberte (left), FSU's president from 1993 to 2003, talks with former FSU fullback Burt Reynolds before a game.

Win No. 239 (Orange Bowl)
Florida State 18, Nebraska 16
January 1, 1994
1993 Season: 12-1

After a nail-biting finish, Bowden secured the national championship that had been eluding him since the late 1970s. While game MVP Ward directed the Florida State offense, Bentley led the Seminoles in scoring with four field goals. His first two kicks pulled FSU to within 7-6 at halftime. In the third quarter, Ward set up William Floyd's 1-yard touchdown run by hitting Knox for a 41-yard completion. Floyd's score put the Seminoles up 12-7. On FSU's next possession, Floyd had a career-long 34-yard run that led to Bentley's third field goal—putting the Seminoles ahead 15-7. Nebraska scored a touchdown in the fourth quarter to pull to within 15-13. The FSU defense, which allowed a 76-yard drive in the final two minutes, drove Nebraska back and forced a field goal that put the Cornhuskers in front 16-15. With the help of two 15-yard Nebraska penalties and a 21-yard pass to Dunn, Ward marched the Seminoles down the field with just over a minute left in the contest. Bowden set up the field goal by calling a time out on a second-and-goal to give Bentley a chance to win the game. Kanell placed the ball down and Bentley nailed his 22-yard field goal with 21 seconds remaining. Before the win became official, however, Bowden endured several tortuous minutes as Nebraska mounted a valiant comeback that ended with a missed 45-yard field goal as time expired. Lost in the championship excitement was the fact that Bowden had moved past Ohio State's Woody Hayes into fifth place in all-time coaching victories.

Scott Bentley's field goal gave Bowden a national championship.

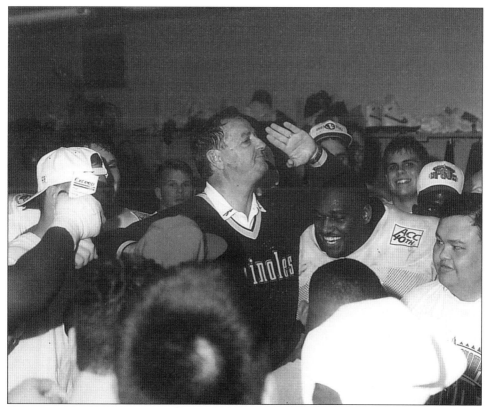

Bowden congratulates the 1993 national champions.

YEAR TWENTY-NINE: THE 1994 SEASON (10-1-1)

Win No. 240
Florida State 41, Virginia 17
September 3, 1994
1994 Season: 1-0

Most preseason publications picked the Seminoles to make a run at their second straight title, with Colorado, Florida, Nebraska, and Notre Dame joining in the fight for the crown. Despite the high predictions, Bowden knew he had to find a replacement for Charlie Ward. Danny Kanell, who had a veteran offensive line, eased Bowden's worries in the home opener as he completed 32-of-48 passes for 330 yards and four touchdowns. Warrick Dunn scored the first FSU touchdown on a 16-yard pass from Kanell. Two additional second-quarter Kanell touchdowns (to Billy Glenn and Kez McCorvey) sent Florida State into halftime leading 20-3. After an interception by All-American Clifton Abraham on the third play of the third quarter set up the second-half scoring, Zack Crockett and Rock Preston each had short scoring runs in the quarter to extend the lead to 34-3 before the reserves finished the game. Sam Cowart led the Seminoles with 13 tackles.

Win No. 241

Florida State 52, Maryland 20

September 10, 1994

1994 Season: 2-0

In the second half at College Park, Florida State's offense exploded and its defense stiffened as the Seminoles outscored the Terrapins 35-0 over the final two quarters. Kanell threw for 427 yards and a fourth-quarter touchdown to McCorvey. Wayne Messam had four receptions for 122 yards. The FSU ground game totaled 279 yards, led by Crockett's 123 yards and 2 scores—the best game by an FSU fullback in eight years. Preston added 2 rushing touchdowns while Dunn, who had 116 yards rushing, had a 25-yard scoring run in the win.

Win No. 242

Florida State 56, Wake Forest 14

September 17, 1994

1994 Season: 3-0

The Seminoles slipped to fourth in the polls, upsetting the players and spelling trouble for the Demon Deacons. FSU built a 49-0 lead in the third quarter in Winston-Salem. The scoring started early, set up by key plays from All-American Derrick Brooks. On Wake Forest's third play, Brooks forced a fumble that James Colzie recovered. The turnover led to a drive that ended on a 15-yard touchdown pass from Kanell to E.G. Green. After a 24-yard scoring run by Crockett, the Seminoles went ahead 21-0 when Brooks blocked a punt that Abraham recovered in the end zone for a touchdown. Brooks, who had a blocked punt, sack, and an interception of a two-point conversion attempt, would go on to a great professional career, winning the 2002 NFL defensive player of the year. Kanell saw limited action in the blowout, as Bowden substituted early with Jon Stark and Thad Busby.

Win No. 243

Florida State 31, North Carolina 18

September 24, 1994

1994 Season: 4-0

Facing the No. 13 Tar Heels at Doak Campbell and in front of an ESPN audience, the third-ranked Seminoles met their toughest opponent yet on the season. Kanell led the way by throwing 3 touchdowns. His first 2 scoring passes opened up a 14-7 lead that the Seminoles would never relinquish. Kanell's first touchdown came on Florida State's opening possession when he hit Melvin Pearsall with a 5-yard touchdown pass. A 46-yard run by Dunn, who had 121 yards, set up Kanell's second score, a 27-yard pass to Andre Cooper. Two third-quarter unanswered touchdowns increased FSU's lead while the defense, led by ACC defensive player of the year Derrick Alexander and Connell Spain, had a solid game forcing 3 turnovers. The Seminoles would have a two-week respite before losing their only game on the season—a 34-20 setback to Miami in the Orange Bowl.

Derrick Alexander earned the 1994 ACC Defensive Player of the Year Award.

Win No. 244

Florida State 17, Clemson 0

October 22, 1994

1994 Season: 5-1

Despite falling to 11th in the polls, the Seminoles had a two-week bye to prepare for their homecoming game against the Tigers. Dunn led the offensive charge with 133 rushing yards and 2 short second-quarter touchdowns. The Seminoles recorded their first and only shutout of the season and their second consecutive game keeping Clemson scoreless. Brooks and Alexander led the Florida State defense, holding the Tigers to 63 yards rushing and 86 yards passing. Dan Mowrey, who took over the kicking duties starting in the second half, nailed a third-quarter field goal to give the game its final score.

Win No. 245

Florida State 59, Duke 20

October 29, 1994

1994 Season: 6-1

Florida State had an explosive second quarter and gained over 600 yards of total offense against the Blue Devils, who had been undefeated and ranked 13th in the country. The win gave the No. 7 Seminoles an ACC record of 22 consecutive conference wins. After a 6-yard touchdown connection between Kanell and Cooper gave the Seminoles a first-quarter lead, FSU scored 32 points in the second quarter to put the game out of reach. The highlights of the second quarter included 2 Crockett touchdown runs and 2 more scoring passes by Kanell. One-yard touchdown runs in the fourth quarter by Crockett and Busby capped off

Warrick Dunn breaks through a hole.

the scoring for the Seminoles. Although McCorvey didn't get involved in the scoring, he had a career day against the Blue Devils with 10 receptions for 207 yards.

Win No. 246
Florida State 41, Georgia Tech 10
November 5, 1994
1994 Season: 7-1
Bowden relied on a run-stopping defense and a run-obsessed offense to defeat the Yellow Jackets at Bobby Dodd Stadium. Georgia Tech ran the ball 27 times, gaining a total of 5 yards against the Seminoles. Florida State, harassing the Yellow Jacket quarterbacks throughout the game, had 5 quarterback sacks and an interception. On offense, Bowden went to the ground game as the sixth-ranked Seminoles ran the ball 43 times for 242 yards and 3 touchdowns. Dunn led the rushing offense, carrying the ball 13 times for a then career-high 174 yards.

Win No. 247
Florida State 23, Notre Dame 16
November 12, 1994
1994 Season: 8-1
Dunn scored with just under three minutes left in the game to give the sixth-ranked Seminoles a close victory in front of an ABC audience and a record-setting crowd of nearly 73,000 in Orlando at the Citrus Bowl. After both teams traded scores through the second

Notre Dame Coach Lou Holtz shares a thought with Bowden.

and third quarters, Florida State led 16-10 at the end of the third quarter on a 28-yard touchdown run by Preston. After the Irish tied the game at 16 with just over five minutes remaining, Kanell led a 68-yard touchdown drive that ended with Dunn's 5-yard score. For the second straight game, Bowden went to his ground attack early and often. The Seminoles rushed the ball 56 times for 377 yards. Dunn gained 163 yards on 29 attempts while Preston added 12 runs for 165 yards.

Win No. 248
Florida State 34, North Carolina State 3
November 19, 1994
1994 Season: 9-1
The Seminoles traveled to Raleigh and found the ground game wide open against the 22nd-ranked Wolfpack. Florida State earned 259 yards on the ground, going over the 200-yard rushing mark for the third consecutive game. Dunn again led all rushers with 122 yards and a touchdown for his third straight 100-yard rushing game. Preston added 81 yards and 2 touchdowns. The Seminoles, who were wearing their garnet pants on the road for the first time in their history, had a 21-point offensive outburst in the second quarter to open a large lead. Kanell threw 2 touchdown passes, a 17-yarder to Philip Riley that ended the first-half scoring and a 25-yard throw that Cooper snared for the final score of the game.

Win No. 249 (Sugar Bowl)
Florida State 23, Florida 17
January 2, 1995
1994 Season: 10-1-1
In the regular season finale against the Gators in Tallahassee, the Seminoles trailed 31-3 in the fourth quarter. But Florida State tied an NCAA Division I-A record for a fourth-quarter comeback by scoring 28 unanswered points to end the game in a tie. Bowden considers the tie game the most memorable of all his games against Florida. Although the season finale ended in a deadlock, the momentum was clearly in FSU's favor as the two teams headed into the Sugar Bowl for a rematch. Florida State, ranked seventh in the country, relied on Dunn to lead the offense. Dunn continued his assault on the fifth-ranked Gators with 182 yards of total offense as the running back completed his stellar year by running, catching, and passing the football to earn game MVP honors. The entire Florida State defense played well as the Seminoles harassed Danny Wuerffel throughout the game, sacking him 5 times. The victory, which was FSU's seventh win in its last nine games against UF, improved Bowden's bowl record to 15-3-1, the best bowl winning percentage in NCAA history.

Sugar Bowl MVP Warrick Dunn discusses his performance with the media.

YEAR THIRTY: THE 1995 SEASON (10–2)

Win No. 250
Florida State 70, Duke 26
September 2, 1995
1995 Season: 1-0
The Seminoles began another season ranked No. 1 in the polls. While the defense struggled without key starters who were injured, the offense sizzled as seven different players scored a touchdown in the trouncing of the Blue Devils in Orlando. Danny Kanell completed 21-of-27 passes for 275 yards and four touchdowns in the first half. While Pooh Bear Williams scored 3 short touchdowns, Rock Preston provided the most exciting play when he rambled through the defense for an 85-yard touchdown. Warrick Dunn rushed for 124 yards, passed for 55 yards, and caught 2 passes for 13 yards.

Win No. 251
Florida State 45, Clemson 26
September 9, 1995
1995 Season: 2-0
The Seminoles struck early on the game's opening drive when Williams rushed for a 2-yard score. Williams added a 6-yard touchdown run on FSU's next possession to give him 5 scores in the previous five quarters. Dunn, who scored 2 touchdowns and was named the ABC player of the game, averaged 15 yards on 12 carries. Kanell threw a 12-yard touchdown pass to E.G. Green and an 11-yard score to Andre Cooper while Scott Bentley added a 28-yard field goal.

Win No. 252
Florida State 77, NC State 17
September 16, 1995
1995 Season: 3-0
Florida State added 2,500 seats to Doak Campbell before the 1995 season and all 72,800 in attendance for the first home game of the season witnessed a game unlike any other. Bowden noted before the season that this team had the potential to be unstoppable, but he never could have dreamed it would all come together so early. Kanell connected on 28 passes for 310 yards, 5 touchdowns, and a school-record 87.5 completion percentage. Thad Busby added 2 touchdown throws to establish a new FSU record of 7 touchdown passes in one game. In addition to the total points, other school records set in this game included 11 total touchdowns and Bentley's 11 extra points.

Win No. 253
Florida State 46, Central Florida 14
September 23, 1995
1995 Season: 4-0
Central Florida coach Gene McDowell, who was an All-American player at FSU and former assistant under Bowden, brought his Knights to Tallahassee to face the No. 1

Seminoles. Williams had a touchdown in each of the first three quarters to lead Florida State. Kanell added 2 touchdown passes, the last of which was an 8-yard scoring strike to Green. Green also scored on a 42-yard reverse in the third quarter to put the game out of reach. The difference in the game according to Bowden was the defensive pressure—including 2 safeties—on UCF and quarterback Daunte Culpepper.

Win No. 254
Florida State 41, Miami 17
October 7, 1995
1995 Season: 5-0
For the first time all season, Bowden's defense was at full stride with the return of Todd Rebol and Daryl Bush from injuries. The two linebackers helped Florida State record 3 sacks and pressure Ryan Clement, who was making his first start, into throwing interceptions to Samari Rolle and James Colzie. The home fans saw FSU gain an early lead when Williams jumped over the line for a 1-yard touchdown. Miami quickly responded when they blocked an FSU punt in the end zone. In the second quarter, the Seminoles built a 31-7 lead with a Bentley field goal, 2 Cooper touchdown receptions, and a 1-yard touchdown run by Dunn.

Win No. 255
Florida State 72, Wake Forest 13
October 14, 1995
1995 Season: 6-0
Although it took almost the entire first quarter to score, the Seminoles eventually put tallies on the board on six consecutive possessions to crush the Demon Deacons. The regulars led Florida State's offense as Kanell threw for 342 yards, Dunn rushed for 112 yards, and Cooper had 5 receptions. Damian Harrell (two touchdown receptions) and Melvin Pearsall (one touchdown reception) also provided clutch plays. For the second week in a row, FSU's defense—led by the eight-tackle performances of Julian Pittman and Andre Wadsworth—was stellar, limiting Wake to 154 total yards compared to the 748 gained by the Seminoles.

Win No. 256
Florida State 42, Georgia Tech 10
October 21, 1995
1995 Season: 7-0
Playing before a home crowd for the fifth consecutive game, the Seminoles extended their unbeaten streak in ACC play to 29 games. The strong-armed Kanell connected on 41-of-51 passes for 302 yards. The Yellow Jackets scored first on a field goal before Dunn capped a five-minute drive with an 8-yard touchdown run. Cooper and Green each caught 3-yard touchdown passes from Kanell before Dee Feaster electrified the crowd with a 64-yard punt return to the 1-yard line. Preston scored on the next play and FSU held a 28-10 lead at the half. In the third quarter, FSU did not put points on the scoreboard, making it the first time all season FSU did not score in a quarter. Cooper and Green each caught

Bowden discusses a play with Assistant Coaches Mickey Andrews (middle) and Chuck Amato (right).

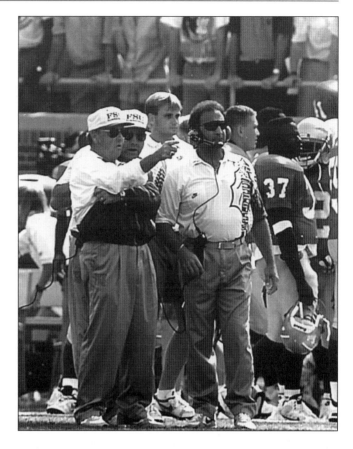

another touchdown pass from Kanell in the fourth quarter to end the scoring. Bush, Wadsworth, Robert Hammond, and Sam Cowart each recorded over 10 tackles to lead the FSU defense.

Win No. 257
Florida State 28, North Carolina 12
November 11, 1995
1995 Season: 8-1

Bowden's unbeaten streak in the ACC came to an end nine days earlier, when Dunn was stopped inches from the goal line in a 33-28 loss at Virginia. On the road against the Tar Heels, the new conference winning streak began as special teams players almost single-handedly won the game. As the Tar Heels attempted to punt on their first possession, Mario Edwards got a hand on the kick and returned it 24 yards for a score. On FSU's very first offensive play, Dunn scampered 43 yards to make the score 14-0. Later in the game Dexter Jackson, who would become the 2003 Super Bowl MVP, blocked an extra point and Peter Boulware blocked a punt to set up another FSU score. While they won the game, FSU experienced a loss, as the truck carrying most of the game equipment caught fire and burned before anything could be saved.

Andre Cooper eludes a tackle for one of his two scores against Maryland in 1995.

Win No. 258
Florida State 59, Maryland 17
November 18, 1995
1995 Season: 9-1
Playing in sunny Tallahassee, Kanell and Busby outgunned Scott Milanovich as the quarterbacks set FSU records for most pass attempts in a game (109) and most passing yards by two teams (876). FSU accounted for 496 passing yards as the Seminoles clinched the conference championship. Cooper and Green were the main targets, as they had been all season. Cooper had a career day with 12 receptions for 182 yards and 2 touchdowns. His second score broke the school record for most touchdown receptions in one season. He finished the season with 15 touchdown catches. Cowart, who finished the year leading the Seminoles with 115 tackles, dominated the game with 14 stops.

Win No. 259 (Orange Bowl)
Florida State 31, Notre Dame 26
January 1, 1996
1995 Season: 10-2
After finishing the regular season 9-2 following a loss at Florida, Bowden took his team to Miami to face the Fighting Irish. Notre Dame led 26-14 in the fourth quarter and Bowden's Seminoles only had 11 minutes to pull out a comeback win. Kanell calmly guided FSU on 2 scoring drives. The first drive of 73 yards ended when Kanell hit Green for an 11-yard score. After a strong defensive stand, Feaster returned a punt 30 yards to position Kanell's game-winning drive of 30 yards that ended when he hit Cooper with a 3-yard touchdown pass with just over six minutes remaining. The successful two-point conversion—another

Kanell-to-Cooper connection—gave the Seminoles a 29-26 lead. Notre Dame attempted to get into field goal range, but the tough FSU defense finished the win by forcing a fumble and safety on the Irish's final two possessions. The win was the 11th straight bowl victory for Bowden and secured a top-four ranking for the ninth consecutive season.

YEAR THIRTY-ONE: THE 1996 SEASON (11–1)

Win No. 260
Florida State 44, Duke 7
September 7, 1996
1996 Season: 1-0
The season began at home with a defensive effort that set up 5 scores. Bowden's defense—led by All-American Reinard Wilson's 16 tackles—held the Blue Devils to a mere 91 yards of total offense. Daryl Bush, Henri Crockett, Vernon Crawford, and Demetro Stephens each had 8 tackles. All-American Peter Boulware added 2.5 sacks on his way to a school single-season record of 19 sacks. Boulware and Wilson benefited from the coaching of Jim Gladden, who—after 20 years as Bowden's linebackers coach—moved to defensive ends coach in 1996. Peter Warrick started the game on a high note by returning the opening kick 48 yards. Thad Busby, making his first start, soon found Andre Cooper in the end zone for a 20-yard touchdown, and the game was never in doubt. After 2 Scott Bentley field goals, Busby hit E.G. Green for a 12-yard touchdown. Just before the half, Dee Feaster returned a punt 59-yards for another touchdown. Early in the second half, Andre Wadsworth forced a fumble that Bush recovered. Moments later Busby handed to Warrick Dunn, who raced around the left end for a 39-yard touchdown and a 34-0 lead. A 1-yard quarterback keeper by Dan Kendra and another Bentley field goal ended the scoring.

Win No. 261
Florida State 51, North Carolina State 17
September 19, 1996
1996 Season: 2-0
The Seminoles traveled to Raleigh for this Thursday-night affair on ESPN and got touchdowns from all three phases of the game. After Bentley hit a field goal, Dunn made an amazing cut and ran 51 yards to put the Seminoles within striking distance. Rolling left, Busby spun and hit Green with a perfect 29-yard touchdown as the first quarter ended. Bowden's special teams and defense eliminated any chance of a comeback. Troy Saunders blocked a punt that Byron Capers recovered for a touchdown and Shevin Smith intercepted a pass and returned it 61 yards for another touchdown. FSU tallied 8 sacks, including two ferocious hits by Boulware.

Win No. 262
Florida State 13, North Carolina 0
September 28, 1996
1996 Season: 3-0
Bobby Bowden knew that this battle between the nation's top two defenses meant that

scoring would be limited and his defense would have to play well. His premonition was true, as the Seminoles had 8 sacks, forced 3 turnovers, and blocked 2 punts and a field goal attempt. Boulware had 3 sacks while Greg Spires added 2. The Tar Heels moved the ball on their first possession and looked to take the early lead with a field goal. But Smith blocked the kick to keep the game scoreless. After trading punts, Dexter Jackson blocked a punt that led to a Bentley field goal and a 3-0 lead in the second quarter. Todd Fordham recovered a fumble during an interception return, leading to a Dunn 11-yard run and the Seminoles went into halftime leading 10-0. Jackson's second punt block put the Seminoles in position for Bentley's 37-yard field goal to end the scoring.

Win No. 263
Florida State 34, Clemson 3
October 5, 1996
1996 Season: 4-0
Thad Busby had a career night against the Tigers at Doak Campbell, throwing for 304 yards and four touchdowns. His first scoring pass was a 37-yarder to Green for the only score of the first quarter. After a Clemson field goal, Busby threw touchdown passes to Green (60 yards), Dunn (27 yards), and Cooper (four yards). Dunn's score came after Warrick made the catch of the season, a diving snare for 50-yards. Dee Feaster completed the scoring when he returned a punt 79 yards in the fourth quarter. Crockett, Wilson, Bush, and Crawford all had over 10 tackles. After the game, Bowden joked that he was upset at his defense as they allowed three first-half points—the only points they allowed in an opening half yet this season.

Win No. 264
Florida State 34, Miami 16
October 12, 1996
1996 Season: 5-0
Bowden had not defeated Miami in the Orange Bowl in 12 years, but Wilson and Dunn made sure that streaked snapped. Wilson sacked Ryan Clement four times, giving the future Cincinnati Bengal a school-record 29 career sacks. FSU went ahead early as Troy Saunders intercepted a pass that led to a Bentley 48-yard field goal. Bowden's defense increased the lead to 10-0 when Crawford forced a fumble that Shevin Smith picked up and returned for a 54-yard score. Dunn next mesmerized the crowd as he took a draw, faked twice and sprinted for a career-long 80-yard touchdown. His score gave the Seminoles a 17-0 first-quarter lead. Miami attempted a comeback, closing the margin to 20-16 at the half, but FSU scored on short touchdown runs by Preston in the third quarter and Busby in the fourth. The defense, led by Wilson's 11 tackles, pitched a second-half shutout to preserve the win.

Win No. 265
Florida State 31, Virginia 24
October 26, 1996
1996 Season: 6-0
The second-ranked Seminoles faced the 13th-ranked Cavaliers in a homecoming battle at

Thad Busby rolls left to elude the defense.

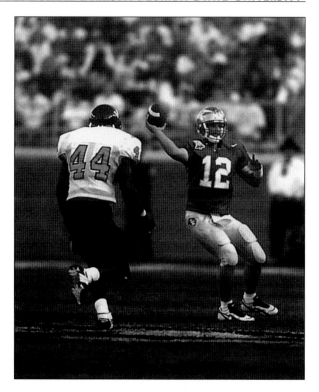

Doak Campbell. Early on it appeared FSU would dominate, as Dunn went through the left side of the line for a 65-yard touchdown and a 7-0 lead. Virginia came back strong and went ahead 17-14 by halftime. The Seminoles regrouped and scored 17 consecutive points in the second half. The Cavaliers, while rallying for one fourth-quarter score, had second-half drives halted by exceptional defensive plays—including Boulware's 3 sacks. One drive died when FSU stopped a fake-punt attempt. Two other drives were ended by interceptions, 1 each by Samari Rolle and James Colzie.

Win No. 266
Florida State 49, Georgia Tech 3
November 2, 1996
1996 Season: 7-0
Playing in Bobby Dodd Stadium and near-freezing temperatures, it took Florida State a quarter to get warmed up before dominating the game. After the Yellow Jackets scored the only points of the first quarter on a field goal, the Seminoles went on to score 28 points in the second quarter—including 21 points over a seven-minute span. FSU scored on a 56-yard interception by Lamont Green, a 6-yard run by Preston, a recovery by Smith in the end zone after a blocked punt by Boulware, and a 38-yard connection between Busby and Cooper. Dunn, who added a 45-yard touchdown run in the third quarter, had 121 rushing yards. Kendra replaced an injured Busby in the fourth quarter and threw a 19-yard touchdown to Warrick and ran for another score. Bush, whose 17 tackles were a career high, led a defense that had now kept its opponent out of the end zone for the third time in seven

155

games. The defense would continue to dominate throughout the season, leading to defensive coordinator Mickey Andrews's winning the Broyles Award.

Win No. 267
Florida State 44, Wake Forest 7
November 9, 1996
1996 Season: 8-0
With five starters injured, Bowden—who himself had early-season back surgery that forced him to coach several games while seated on the sidelines—relied on young reserves to dismantle the Demon Deacons at the Citrus Bowl in Orlando. With Busby nursing a fractured wrist, Bowden turned to Kendra for his first career start. The freshman, whose father (Dan Kendra Sr.) Bowden had coached at West Virginia, responded by throwing for 281 yards and leading FSU to touchdowns on four of the first five possessions. His 3 touchdown passes clinched the fifth straight ACC title for the Seminoles. Dunn scored 2 rushing touchdowns early. Boulware, who had 2 sacks, set up Dunn's second score when he recovered a fumble that Wilson had forced. Warrick also made the most of his first start replacing Cooper, who was on the bench due to an injury he suffered in warm-ups. Warrick caught 3 passes for 72 yards, including a 42-yard bomb from Kendra.

Win No. 268
Florida State 54, Southern Mississippi 14
November 16, 1996
1996 Season: 9-0
The Golden Eagles came to Tallahassee with a Top-25 ranking and a highly regarded offense. While Southern Miss did score first, the Seminoles quickly put the game out of reach with an offensive juggernaut that accumulated 548 total yards. Dunn scored from the 4-yard line to tie the game. On FSU's next possession, Laveranues Coles scored the first touchdown of his career when he caught an 8-yard pass from Busby. After another Golden Eagle touchdown tied the game at 14 early in the second quarter, the Seminoles went on to score 40 unanswered points. The highlight of the second-half scoring was a 77-yard connection between Busby and Dunn. The touchdown gave Dunn 47 for his career, breaking the FSU record set by Greg Allen.

Win No. 269
Florida State 48, Maryland 10
November 23, 1996
1996 Season: 10-0
Dunn, Warrick, Bentley, and the Seminole defense starred once again. Warrick put Florida State in the lead for good in the first quarter when he made the catch of the year. He knocked a Busby pass out of the defenders hands before reaching with one hand to snare the 44-yard touchdown. Bentley connected on a career-long 49-yard field goal as the first half ended to give FSU a 24-10 lead. Dunn, who rushed for 109 yards to break Allen's career rushing yards record, finished the year with 3,959 yards rushing for his career. The defense, which had 8 sacks, including 3 by Wilson and 2 by Lamont Green,

held the Terrapins to negative rushing yards while providing Bowden a 10-win season for the 10th straight year.

Win No. 270
Florida State 24, Florida 21
November 30, 1996
1996 Season: 11-0

With the excitement of a No. 1 (Florida) vs. No. 2 (Florida State) match-up before a record crowd (80,932) at Doak Campbell, Bowden ranks this victory as "the greatest" in the in-state rivalry series. Only three times in college football history did two undefeated teams meet in a season finale. The top-ranked FSU defense dominated throughout the game, holding the Gators to 81 rushing yards while recording 6 sacks. UF quarterback Danny Weurffel was knocked to the ground 25 times while throwing 3 interceptions and tying a career high for incompletions. The defense—led by Wilson, who had 7 tackles and 1 sack to establish a school record with 34.5 career sacks—set up Florida State's first score when Smith intercepted a pass on Florida's first possession. Bentley hit a 29-yard field goal to begin a 17-0 first-quarter run by the Seminoles. The Gators came back with 14 unanswered points in the second quarter. Later, Florida missed 2 field goals that would have tied the game. After the second miss, Busby led a 75-yard drive that ended when Pooh Bear Williams scored the second of his 2 short rushing touchdowns. Dunn rushed for a career-best 185 yards while Warrick made several amazing plays that kept FSU drives alive. However, the biggest play may have been a Boulware punt block that led to Williams's first rushing score. The victory gave the Seminoles a perfect regular season and an invitation to the national championship game against the Gators in the Sugar Bowl. Florida won the

*Greg Spires records one of
FSU's 6 quarterback sacks.*

rematch, and the Seminoles finished third in the polls, marking the 10th straight season they finished in the top four. Bowden ended the outstanding year by being named the Home Depot College Football National Coach of the Year.

YEAR THIRTY–TWO: THE 1997 SEASON (11–1)

Win No. 271
Florida State 14, Southern California 7
September 6, 1997
1997 Season: 1-0
The Seminoles, in their season opener, escaped with the win thanks to a swarming defense and a 97-yard scoring drive in the fourth quarter. Dee Feaster, who led all rushers with 93 yards, scored on a 3-yard touchdown run to give the Seminoles a win in their first trip to the Los Angeles Coliseum. Although the FSU offense failed to find a rhythm, Dan Kendra found the end zone on a 1-yard touchdown run in the first quarter for Florida State's only other score. The FSU defense, led by linebackers Sam Cowart and Daryl Bush, allowed only 184 total yards by the Trojans, including 25 yards on 33 carries. Cowart, who had missed the entire 1996 season with a knee injury, returned to action with 19 tackles.

Win No. 272
Florida State 50, Maryland 7
September 13, 1997
1997 Season: 2-0
Thad Busby combined with two other quarterbacks for 461 yards and 5 touchdowns in the home opener. Busby played in just the first half, where he threw for 308 yards and 2

Bowden and Maryland Coach Ron Vanderlinden talk before the game.

touchdowns. Both of Busby's scoring throws were to wide receiver E.G. Green, who had 6 catches for 188 yards. Dan Kendra played the third quarter while freshman Chris Weinke took the first snap of his Florida State career in the fourth quarter. Bowden's defense played its second strong game, giving up 57 yards passing and 48 yards rushing. Bill Gramatica made 1 short field goal while Sebastian Janikowski nailed both of his field goal attempts.

Win No. 273
Florida State 35, Clemson 28
September 20, 1997
1997 Season: 3-0
Bowden picked up his 200th Florida State victory thanks to Peter Warrick's breakout game at "Death Valley." After touring the stadium with Jeff Bowden before the game and finding out that it was here that Deion Sanders exploded onto the national scene nine years earlier, Warrick had one of his best collegiate days as he went for 372 total yards, including 8 receptions for 249 yards and 2 touchdowns. Busby, who threw for 332 yards, hit Warrick with a 48-yard strike in the third quarter to give the Seminoles their first lead of the game. Warrick also had an 80-yard touchdown reception in the fourth quarter to extend the FSU lead. In addition to his work as a wide receiver, he also returned a punt 90 yards for a touchdown in the fourth quarter.

Win No. 274
Florida State 47, Miami 0
October 4, 1997
1997 Season: 4-0
Bowden approached games against Miami with trepidation. If there was one team that was close to having the legendary coach's number, it was the Hurricanes. But at home in 1997, it was all Florida State as five different Seminoles scored a touchdown and Janikowski hit 2 field goals. The FSU defense was the real story, as it held the Hurricanes to minus-33 yards on the ground. Florida State also stifled the UM air attack by intercepting 3 passes and holding Ryan Clement and Scott Covington to 164 yards passing. The victory was Florida State's most lopsided win against the Hurricanes and the second biggest shutout loss in Miami history. The biggest shutout was a 52-0 defeat in 1927 at the hands of Howard College. "I didn't know that," said Bowden when informed of the record. He joked with reporters that he would have gone for another touchdown if he had known it would have moved him in front of his alma mater.

Win No. 275
Florida State 51, Duke 27
October 11, 1997
1997 Season: 5-0
Before Duke scored 3 late touchdowns, the Florida State defense was actually outscoring the host Blue Devils. Sam Cowart scored the first defensive touchdown when he recovered a fumble—forced by Tony Bryant's sack—and returned it for a 24-yard score. A second defensive score came when Derrick Gibson returned a blocked punt for a 1-yard

touchdown. Offensive tackle Tra Thomas opened holes for 38 FSU running plays. Davy Ford and Travis Minor each scored a touchdown and were two of nine Seminoles who gained rushing yards. In the passing game, Warrick had another great outing with 5 receptions for 134 yards and a touchdown.

Win No. 276
Florida State 38, Georgia Tech 0
October 18, 1997
1997 Season: 6-0
For the second time in three games, the FSU defense recorded a shutout. This time the defenders held the visiting Yellow Jackets to 53 yards rushing and only 91 yards passing while recording 5 sacks. Georgia Tech quarterback Joe Hamilton was frustrated throughout the game, throwing for only 83 yards. A third-quarter interception by Tay Cody sealed the fate of the Yellow Jackets, and on the very next play Busby hit Green for a 66-yard touchdown for a 21-0 lead. The final score of the game came when Kendra hit Laveranues Coles for a 47-yard touchdown with two minutes remaining. That touchdown would be Kendra's last as a quarterback, as he asked Bowden to switch him to fullback in 1998 after he was injured in spring drills.

Win No. 277
Florida State 47, Virginia 21
October 25, 1997
1997 Season: 7-0
Two years earlier, the Seminoles had traveled to Scott Stadium and suffered their first ACC loss. But in 1997, FSU scored 3 touchdowns on its first five offensive plays to show an ESPN national television audience that the Cavaliers would not be giving the third-ranked Seminoles their second conference setback. Minor had a field day in his first collegiate start, running for 155 yards and scoring 3 touchdowns. On Florida State's first possession of the game, Minor scampered for an 87-yard score. Busby then hit Warrick for a 30-yard score on the first play after a Virginia three-and-out. On FSU's fifth play of the game, Busby helped the Seminoles build a 21-0 lead when he connected with Green for a 74-yard touchdown. The FSU defense did the rest, holding the Cavaliers to minus-nine yards rushing. Andre Wadsworth had 3 of Florida State's record 9 quarterback sacks.

Win No. 278
Florida State 48, North Carolina State 35
November 1, 1997
1997 Season: 8-0
The Seminoles jumped out to a 27-0 first quarter lead in the homecoming game against the Wolfpack. Busby had his best day as a Seminole, completing 26-of-36 passes for 463 yards and 5 touchdowns. Green caught 3 of the scoring passes and had 184 receiving yards. Minor crossed the goal line 3 times, catching 2 touchdowns and running for another.

Win No. 279
Florida State 20, North Carolina 3
November 8, 1997
1997 Season: 9-0
Coach Bowden, who turned 68 on the day of the game, wondered before the season who might step in for departed All-America defensive ends Peter Boulware and Reinard Wilson. Replacements were soon discovered in Greg Spires and Andre Wadsworth, who had moved from middle guard to end. As the season progressed, the defensive line meshed into an outstanding unit with the added emergence of Jerry Johnson, Larry Smith, and Julian Pittman. Against the fifth-ranked Tar Heels, in what was considered the biggest game in ACC history at the time, the FSU defensive line had a brilliant game as Spires collected 4 sacks and Wadsworth added 3. The second-ranked Seminoles had 9 sacks while forcing four turnovers and limiting the Tar Heels to minus-28 yards rushing and only 101 yards passing. Wadsworth, whose performance at Chapel Hill was seen by an ESPN national audience, would finish the year with 16 sacks while being honored as yet another consensus All-American.

Win No. 280
Florida State 58, Wake Forest 7
November 15, 1997
1997 Season: 10-0
Bowden claimed his sixth-straight conference title in this blowout at Doak Campbell. Green and Melvin Pearsall each went over the 100-yard receiving mark with 120 yards and 114 yards, respectively. Green had 2 touchdown receptions while Pearsall hauled in a 45-yard scoring pass from Busby, who threw for 390 yards and four touchdowns in the win.

E.G. Green scored 2 touchdowns against Wake Forest.

Tony Bryant returned an interception 19 yards for a touchdown that capped off Florida State's first-quarter scoring at 28-0. In the third quarter, with the Seminoles ahead 45-0, Janikowski hit a 56-yard field goal to set an FSU record. After blowing out the Demon Deacons, the top-ranked Seminoles faced the Gators at Ben Hill Griffin Stadium. Florida won the game 32-29, overcoming a 149-yard rushing performance by Minor, who was later named the ACC Rookie of the Year. The other major conference honor went to Bowden, who picked up his second ACC Coach of the Year award. He had also won that title in 1993.

Win No. 281 (Sugar Bowl)
Florida State 31, Ohio State 14
January 1, 1998
1997 Season: 11-1
The Seminoles, despite dropping out of championship contention with the loss at Florida, had little trouble ending the year on a high note against John Cooper's Buckeyes. Florida State jumped out to a 21-3 halftime lead behind a 27-yard touchdown pass from Busby to Green along with a 9-yard touchdown run by Busby and a 1-yard scoring plunge by William McCray. Green was voted the MVP with 7 catches for 176 yards. The Seminoles finished their scoring when Janikowski added a 35-yard field goal and McCray ran in his second 1-yard touchdown. With the win, Bowden secured his 17th career bowl victory and his 11th triumph in the last 12 bowls. The Sugar Bowl victory moved the Seminoles to third in the polls and kept their record streak of top-four finishes in the AP poll alive at 11 seasons.

Bowden receives the Sugar Bowl Trophy.

YEAR THIRTY-THREE: THE 1998 SEASON (11-2)

Win No. 282
Florida State 23, Texas A&M 14
August 31, 1998
1998 Season: 1-0
The Seminoles had a 10-0 first-quarter lead, only to go into halftime down 14-10. After Sebastian Janikowski hit his second of 3 field goals, Florida State went ahead for good at the end of the third quarter when Chris Weinke connected with Peter Warrick for a 9-yard touchdown. Weinke ended his first career start completing 21-of-36 passes for 207 yards and a touchdown. Warrick began his junior campaign with 9 catches for 106 yards. Bowden also went to a running attack often as the Seminoles ran the ball 47 times in the Kickoff Classic played in the Meadowlands. Travis Minor carried a school-record 34 times for 152 yards and a touchdown. The Florida State defense, led by seniors Lamont Green and Dexter Jackson, held the Aggies to 33 yards on the ground and 133 through the air.

Win No. 283
Florida State 62, Duke 13
September 19, 1998
1998 Season: 2-1
A week earlier at North Carolina State, the Seminoles lost for only the second time in 49 conference games. The 24-7 upset appeared to eliminate Florida State from any possibility of a national championship. The startled Seminoles had trouble regrouping against the Blue Devils as Duke led 7-0 after the first quarter and later tied the game 10-10 in the second quarter. FSU eventually caught fire and—starting with a 97-yard kickoff return for a touchdown by Laveranues Coles—scored 42 unanswered points. Weinke completed only 11 passes, but 3 of his throws were for touchdowns. Warrick caught two of the scores while Minor pulled in the third and ran for another. Jeff Chaney had 2 short touchdown runs and William McCray added a third.

Win No. 284
Florida State 30, Southern California 10
September 26, 1998
1998 Season: 3-1
Hurricane Georges appeared to be heading for Tallahassee and athletics department officials began making plans to postpone the game. But the storm dumped only rain and, instead of facing the wrath of Mother Nature, the USC passing attack faced the talented Florida State defense. FSU defenders allowed only 23 passing yards. Dexter Jackson had an interception, and his defensive colleagues collected four sacks in the win. Weinke threw touchdown passes to Warrick and Ron Dugans, while Jeff Chaney came off the bench for an injured Minor and ran for 89 yards and a touchdown.

Win No. 285
Florida State 24, Maryland 10
October 3, 1998
1998 Season: 4-1
The Seminoles established a 13-0 first-quarter lead and stayed ahead for the win as the defense held the Terrapins to 197 total yards. Tay Cody had an interception and the defense put points on the scoreboard when Roland Seymour sacked Randall Jones in the end zone. Weinke hit Coles with a 38-yard touchdown for the first score of the game. Janikowski, who was having an All-American season, provided the rest of the scoring as he tied Bill Capece's school record of 5 field goals in a game. With Minor still injured, Chaney started and had his best day as a Seminole, rushing 30 times for 133 yards.

Win No. 286
Florida State 26, Miami 14
October 10, 1998
1998 Season: 5-1
Although Bowden came into this game having won three straight games against the Hurricanes, over his career he had lost more games (14) to Miami than any other team. His defensive unit in 1998 was not about to let the legendary coach pick up his 15th loss as the Seminoles recorded 7 sacks, an interception, and a safety while holding the Hurricanes to 69 yards rushing. Tommy Polley intercepted a pass and Seymour recorded a safety for the

Chris Weinke's pump fake caught Miami off guard.

second consecutive game. Weinke, who threw his first 300-yard game while throwing touchdown passes to Warrick and Marvin Minnis, became the first FSU quarterback to throw a touchdown pass in the Orange Bowl since Brad Johnson in 1990.

Win No. 287

Florida State 48, Clemson 0

October 17, 1998

1998 Season: 6-1

Bowden put together a complete game plan against the visiting Tigers as his defense allowed only 129 yards of total offense and his offense scored 6 touchdowns. The defense put the scoring in motion when Mario Edwards recovered a fumble that led to Weinke's first of four touchdown passes. Weinke, who had his second consecutive 300-yard passing game with 302 yards, threw touchdown passes to Coles (40 yards), Warrick (48 yards), Dugans (12 yards), and Minnis (15 yards). Chaney added a 41-yard touchdown run, while backup quarterback Marcus Outzen completed the scoring with a 2-yard rushing score. Janikowski hit 2 field goals, the first of which was a season-high 53-yard kick in the second quarter. After Clemson ended the season, the Tigers hired Tommy Bowden from Tulane, where he had just completed an 11-0 season.

Win No. 288

Florida State 34, Georgia Tech 7

October 24, 1998

1998 Season: 7-1

After allowing a long scoring drive on Georgia Tech's first possession, the Florida State defense toughened and shut out the Yellow Jackets the rest of the game. FSU held Joe Hamilton, the ACC's leading passer, to 8 completions for 56 yards. Warrick put together an outstanding all-around performance as the visiting Seminoles scored 34 unanswered points. The junior wideout, who had a dazzling reverse that went for a 16-yard touchdown in the fourth quarter, also caught 2 touchdowns and returned 2 punts. Coles saw some action at running back and gained 60 of his 82 rushing yards on a touchdown run with under three minutes remaining.

Win No. 289

Florida State 39, North Carolina 13

October 31, 1998

1998 Season: 8-1

Minor, healthy and starting for the first time in over a month, scored 2 first-half touchdowns to give the Seminoles a 16-3 lead on Halloween night at Doak Campbell. The sophomore led the Seminoles in rushing with 76 yards while Janikowski led the scoring with four field goals on four attempts. Weinke had his third 300-yard performance as the sophomore threw for 338 yards, including fourth-quarter touchdowns to Coles and Warrick. Coles ended the game with 5 receptions for 120 yards while Warrick had 3 catches for 125 yards, including a 56-yard touchdown. The defense, led by Corey Simon and Polley, held the Tar Heels to 75 yards rushing.

Win No. 290

Florida State 45, Virginia 14

November 7, 1998

1998 Season: 9-1

After Weinke took a hard hit that fractured his vertebrae late in the second quarter, Bowden relied on Outzen to lead the offense through the rest of the season. Before the season-ending sack, Weinke had thrown a 79-yard scoring pass to Warrick in the first quarter and run for a 1-yard touchdown in the second quarter. Dexter Jackson, who led the FSU defense in holding Aaron Brooks to 96 passing yards, intercepted 2 passes, the first setting up Weinke's short scoring run. Outzen led the Seminoles to 24 unanswered points in the second half behind a Janikowski field goal and rushing touchdowns by Minor, Chaney, and Raymont Skaggs.

Win No. 291

Florida State 24, Wake Forest 7

November 14, 1998

1998 Season: 10-1

Mario Edwards picked off four passes, matching the interception total the Seminoles had the week before against the Cavaliers. His four interceptions, which tied an ACC record, are the most by an FSU player in a single game. Outzen, who threw for 164 yards in his first career start, began the Seminole scoring with a 1-yard touchdown run at Groves Stadium. Janikowski added a field goal, and Minor ran for 2 more touchdowns as the Seminoles struggled for the win in their first full game without Weinke at the helm.

Win No. 292

Florida State 23, Florida 12

November 21, 1998

1998 Season: 11-1

Although Outzen and Warrick dominated the headlines, it was the FSU defense that secured the win. The fourth-ranked Gators, held scoreless in the second half, were limited to their lowest offensive output (204 yards) in eight years. Florida's Doug Johnson completed only 13-of-36 passes while throwing interceptions to Edwards, Reggie Durden, and Sean Key. Outzen had the best game of his career, throwing for 167 yards and a touchdown while running the ball 17 times for 61 yards. The fifth-ranked Seminoles took their first lead early in the third quarter when Warrick ran 32 yards to the end zone after catching a pass that bounced off a Florida defender. Early in the fourth quarter, Florida State extended its lead to 20-12 when Warrick stopped his reverse and found Dugans for a 46-yard touchdown pass. Janikowski completed the scoring with his third field goal of the game. Following the triumph over the Gators, the Seminoles went to the championship game for their first of three consecutive title-game invitations. Although they lost 23-16 to Tennessee in the Fiesta Bowl, there was promise of a bright future for the 69-year-old Bowden and his Seminole Nation when Warrick announced four days after the loss to the Volunteers that he would return for his senior season.

YEAR THIRTY-FOUR: THE 1999 SEASON (12-0)

Win No. 293
Florida State 41, Louisiana Tech 7
August 29, 1999
1999 Season: 1-0

Two things were certain after FSU's season-opening win: Chris Weinke's spinal surgery was successful and Peter Warrick was the most exciting player in college football. The 72,702 fans at Doak Campbell might have held their collective breath each of the five times Weinke hit the ground, but there was no reason for concern according to the quarterback, who completed 20-of-32 passes for 242 yards and 2 touchdowns. "For me to get hit was not a big deal," said Weinke. *ESPN The Magazine* put Warrick on the cover of its college football preseason issue with the title, "It's war and Peter Warrick is FSU's bomb." The senior wideout, who had 9 catches for 121 yards, was magical after taking a handoff from Weinke before the half. The senior wideout darted from sideline-to-sideline twice before shaking six defenders who seemingly had him down. Bowden later joked that he drew up the play and Warrick was just following directions. Reporters noted that Bowden's 1999 squad had the talent to go wire-to-wire as No. 1 in the nation. In addition to Warrick, the team had three other returning All-Americans in Corey Simon, Jason Whitaker, and Sebastian Janikowski.

Peter Warrick reverses his direction for a dramatic touchdown against Louisiana Tech.

Win No. 294

Florida State 41, Georgia Tech 35

September 11, 1999

1999 Season: 2-0

When Warrick returned for one more season, the senior assumed a significant leadership position on the team. His phrase, "TEAM—It's not about me," was printed on the practice shirts that the players wore under their equipment. While Warrick led the Seminoles, Georgia Tech's Joe Hamilton was billed as the most exciting quarterback in the country. He may have been unless you count Warrick as a quarterback. Bowden used Warrick under center for one play and he scored the game's first points on a 17-yard draw. The 10th-ranked Yellow Jackets kept up with the potent Seminoles as the teams scored on seven straight possessions. Although the score was close throughout the contest, Florida State never trailed. Dan Kendra caught a touchdown pass in his first career start at fullback. Sebastian Janikowski kicked long field goals of 46 and 45 yards to secure the win.

Win No. 295

Florida State 42, North Carolina State 11

September 18, 1999

1999 Season: 3-0

The Seminoles were stacked and balanced on all facets of Bowden's team in 1999. In the few times when the offense was not prolific—as in the game against the Wolfpack when the Seminoles managed only 378 yards—Bowden could rely on his defense and special teams. Janikowski kicked 5 field goals to single-handedly outscore the Wolfpack and lead Florida State to its third straight home win. Defensive touchdowns on an interception by Abdul Howard and a forced fumble by Jamal Reynolds that David Warren recovered put the game well out of reach. The win was Bowden's 100th in the 1990s, as FSU became the fifth school in college football history to win 100 games in one decade. The Seminoles finished the decade with 109 wins, the most of any school over that period. By never falling below fourth in the final AP poll at the end of each year during the 1990s, FSU's high-performance consistency surpassed Notre Dame's run in the 1940s and Oklahoma's dominance in the 1950s.

Win No. 296

Florida State 42, North Carolina 10

September 25, 1999

1999 Season: 4-0

Bowden's offense, which had struggled the week earlier, exploded for 28 points in the first seven minutes against the Tar Heels. Travis Minor started the scoring with a 14-yard touchdown run. After North Carolina ran two plays, Jerry Johnson forced a fumble that set up another Minor score. Sean Key then intercepted a pass and returned it for a touchdown. Although the Tar Heels did get a first down on their next drive, a punt four plays later was returned 75 yards for a score by Warrick, who seemingly had his name on the Heisman trophy at this point in the season. After the win, Bowden signed his eighth contract with FSU, which called for him to receive $6.3 million over five years.

Chris Weinke was the leader of the 1999 National Championship team.

Win No. 297
Florida State 51, Duke 23
October 2, 1999
1999 Season: 5-0
Coming into the game, Florida State was averaging 42 points a contest. The offensive output against the Blue Devils at Alltel Stadium in Jacksonville gave Bowden his highest scoring game of the season. Warrick, in addition to catching 3 first-quarter touchdowns, threw a 35-yard touchdown pass to Laveranues Coles. Bowden had hoped to rest his starters, but when the second and third string allowed 13 points, he put the regulars back in to end any Duke thoughts of a comeback. Weinke returned and quickly threw a perfect 80-yard scoring pass to Ron Dugans, who hauled in 5 passes for 141 yards.

Win No. 298
Florida State 31, Miami 21
October 9, 1999
1999 Season: 6-0
The top-ranked Seminoles, riding a 43-game unbeaten streak at home, looked up at a 21-21 scoreboard going into halftime against the 19th-ranked Hurricanes. But the defense

toughened and recorded its second, second-half shutout of the season. On offense, Minor ran for 125 yards while Weinke spread his passes around to 11 different Seminoles. Minor's only score, a 2-yard run in the fourth quarter, clinched the game. Bowden, who rarely used his tight ends as receivers, caught Miami by surprise when he called for a play that resulted in an 18-yard touchdown reception by Ryan Sprague to tie the game in the second quarter. The Seminoles—with their fifth straight win over the Hurricanes— continued to roll under the leadership of Weinke. The junior signal caller, who had little trouble finding replacements for the suspended Warrick and departed Coles, completed 23 passes for 332 yards.

Win No. 299
Florida State 33, Wake Forest 10
October 16, 1999
1999 Season: 7-0
With Coles off the team and Warrick still suspended, the Seminoles struggled on offense against the Demon Deacons. But Florida State won its 28th straight home contest. After Wake Forest hit an early field goal, Janikowski connected on 3 first-half field goals. Weinke found Atrews Bell in the end zone for third-quarter touchdown passes of 12 and 9 yards. After Tommy Polley recovered a Demon Deacon fumble, the Seminoles were ready to score

Clemson Coach Tommy Bowden (right) shares a moment with Bowden before his father's 300th win.

again. Bowden, who frequently placed a variety of skill players under center to catch defenses off guard, had Anquan Boldin line up as quarterback. The freshman wide receiver rewarded the move with a 2-yard touchdown sneak.

Win No. 300
Florida State 17, Clemson 14
October 23, 1999
1999 Season: 8-0
This game was historic on two accounts. Bowden recorded his 300th victory, only the sixth Division I-A coach to accomplish that feat. He also coached against his son Tommy, marking the first time in college football that a father and son had faced each other. Warrick, who was returning to action for the first time in three weeks, found a hostile, record-breaking crowd of 86,200 at "Death Valley." Although he was rusty, the senior All American helped open the offense as he caught 11 passes for 121 yards. "It was great to have him out there," said Weinke, who threw for 254 yards. "He's the best football player in college right now. This whole team was excited to have him back."

Win No. 301
Florida State 35, Virginia 10
October 30, 1999
1999 Season: 9-0
Florida State fell behind for the fourth consecutive game, but a strong defense, impressive second half by Weinke, and more Warrick highlights gave the Seminoles the win. Two touchdown receptions by Marvin Minnis put the Seminoles ahead 14-10 before two electrifying plays put the game out of reach. The first was set up by Corey Simon, who, dropping back into coverage, read the play perfectly and intercepted his first career pass. Minor then took a handoff from Weinke and eluded several defenders for a 66-yard touchdown run at the end of the third quarter. Five minutes later, Warrick caught a pass on the right side, and, after seemingly standing still, made four defenders miss before racing 50 yards for another eye-opening score that helped Bowden clinch yet another ACC title.

Win No. 302
Florida State 49, Maryland 10
November 13, 1999
1999 Season: 10-0
Florida State's 1999 senior class was one of the most dominating classes in the history of college football. Their victory over the Terrapins secured their place in the record books as the first Seminole class to go undefeated at home. While they didn't yet have a national title, they were only two wins away from that accomplishment. Before the game, Bowden honored all his seniors, including captains Simon and Todd Frier. Then, seniors Warrick and Dugans combined to receive 5 of Weinke's 6 touchdown passes to lead the offensive charge in their last home game. The elusive Warrick hauled in 3 touchdowns while Dugans caught 2. With his 134 receiving yards, Warrick ended the game with a career total of 3,427 receiving yards to break Torry Holt's ACC record. Warrick's 3 scores gave him 32 career

touchdown catches to break E.G. Green's school record. Clevan Thomas kept the Maryland offense off the field with 2 of Florida State's four interceptions.

Win No. 303
Florida State 30, Florida 23
November 20, 1999
1999 Season: 11-0
Bowden one-upped Steve Spurrier's two-quarterback system when he lined up four different players (Weinke, Outzen, Warrick, and Kendra) under center in the first nine minutes of the road victory. The Seminoles knew a victory would put them in the championship game but had to wait until the last tick of the clock to celebrate. The Seminoles led by a touchdown going into the fourth quarter thanks to Warrick (touchdown), Janikowski (three field goals, including a 54 yarder), and Polley (blocked punt). Jean Jeune prevented the Gators from tying the game when he intercepted a Doug Johnson pass at the 2-yard line. Capitalizing on the turnover, Weinke lofted a perfect spiral that Minnis caught for a 27-yard score and a 14-point lead. Florida was able to mount a comeback that included 1 touchdown, but when Johnson's Hail Mary hit the ground as time expired, Bowden was just one win away from the perfect season that had eluded him for 33 years as a head coach at the Division I-A level.

Win No. 304 (Sugar Bowl)
Florida State 46, Virginia Tech 29
January 4, 2000
1999 Season: 12-0
Bowden had done everything possible as a coach, except go undefeated. Warrick and

Peter Warrick was awarded the Sugar Bowl MVP Award to conclude an incredible 1999 season.

Weinke made sure that their coach accomplished the feat as they put on spectacular performances to defeat Michael Vick and his Hokie teammates in the Superdome. Although the Heisman Trophy was awarded to Ron Dayne of Wisconsin, game MVP Warrick's Sugar Bowl record 20 points (three touchdowns and a two-point conversion) proved he was the most exciting player in the land. After Vick fumbled near the goal line, Weinke threw a perfect pass to Warrick for a 64-yard touchdown to start the scoring. FSU's defense, not to be outdone, forced a punt on the next possession that Polley blocked and Jeff Chaney returned for six points. After a Virginia Tech score, Dugans caught a 63-yard touchdown pass from Weinke. Then, with Warrick back to return a punt, the Hokies purposely punted in front of Warrick, who looked as though he would not attempt a return. At the last minute Warrick grabbed the ball and eluded the defense for a 59-yard touchdown. The senior wide receiver, however, saved his best for last. He cut in front of a defender to tip a pass from Weinke only to make a spectacular one-handed catch for a 43-yard score. The reception was featured on the cover of *Sports Illustrated*. The win gave Bowden his second national title, and the Seminoles became the first team in college football history to go wire-to-wire ranked No. 1.

YEAR THIRTY-FIVE: THE 2000 SEASON (11-2)

Win No. 305
Florida State 29, Brigham Young 3
August 26, 2000
2000 Season: 1-0
LaVell Edwards began his final year of coaching by facing Bowden's dominating defense and explosive offense at the Pigskin Classic in Jacksonville. Defensive end Jamal Reynolds, whose pressure resulted in a safety and 2 sacks, led the defensive attack that collected 5 sacks and forced four turnovers. Weinke, who surprised fans and coaches by returning for his senior season, directed the offense by hitting eight different Seminoles. The signal caller, who had 318 passing yards with career highs in completions (32) and attempts (50), threw touchdown passes to Atrews Bell and junior-college transfer Javon Walker. Bell had a 3-yard touchdown reception and a 6-yard touchdown run. Marvin Minnis added career highs in receptions (nine) and receiving yardage (137).

Win No. 306
Florida State 26, Georgia Tech 21
September 9, 2000
2000 Season: 2-0
Florida State faced an unexpected close call in Atlanta as the defense stopped a strong comeback by halting Georgia Tech's go-ahead scoring drive late in the fourth quarter. The Seminoles, behind 175 first-quarter passing yards by Weinke, built a 12-0 lead. But the Yellow Jackets scored 15 unanswered points to take a 15-12 lead heading into the fourth quarter. Weinke then directed 2 touchdown drives in the final quarter to pull out the win. The 28-year-old quarterback had a career night with 443 yards, including a 63-yard touchdown pass to Walker and a 30-yard scoring throw to Robert Morgan. His passing

performance against the Yellow Jackets moved him ahead of Danny Kanell and Gary Huff as the Florida State passing record holder with 6,433 yards.

Win No. 307
Florida State 63, North Carolina 14
September 16, 2000
2000 Season: 3-0
Tar Heel quarterback Ronald Curry's exceptional running and passing ability had FSU coaches concerned as to how their defense would play against the man Bowden referred to as "a right-handed Michael Vick." The worry turned out to be unnecessary as the second-ranked Seminoles used their defensive line pressure and overall team speed to limit Curry to minus-24 yards rushing and 235 yards passing. The Florida State defense had 5 sacks and forced four turnovers that led to scores. The defense even scored when Chris Hope returned a second-quarter fumble 14 yards for a touchdown. Hope joined nine other Seminoles who scored in the win. Weinke threw 2 touchdowns each to Minnis and Bell. Minnis had 5 receptions for 132 yards. The Seminoles, led by Minor's 112 rushing yards, ran for 194 yards against the nation's top-ranked run defense.

Travis Minor led FSU with 112 rushing yards against North Carolina.

Win No. 308
Florida State 31, Louisville 0
September 23, 2000
2000 Season: 4-0
Coming into the season, defensive coordinator Mickey Andrews told his players that he'd be happy if they could hold their opponents under 15 points each game. The second-ranked Seminoles held the highly potent Cardinals to 3 yards rushing and a season-low 210 yards of total offense in recording Florida State's first shutout in 23 games. Dave Ragone led the Louisville offense that was ranked 21st in total offense with an average of 435 yards a contest. However, the visiting Cardinals were shut out for the first time in eight years when the Seminoles put together a remarkable fourth-quarter goal-line stand. "That's when you have to buckle down and play your hardest," said Reynolds, who recorded 2 sacks. Tommy Polley, who forced a fumble that led to a Florida State score, also returned his second career interception for a touchdown in the second quarter to extend the scoring streak by the FSU defense to five straight games.

Win No. 309
Florida State 59, Maryland 7
September 28, 2000
2000 Season: 5-0
Former Seminole defensive stars Peter Boulware and Corey Simon were on the sidelines for the game in College Park. So, it was only natural that the defense set the tone for a blowout. Reynolds recorded his second safety of the year as the Florida State defense increased its scoring streak to six games. Later, Chris Hope intercepted a pass that led to fullback William McCray's second short touchdown run and a 25-0 lead. McCray had an outstanding year after an injury forced him to miss most of the previous season and allowed for the emergence of Dan Kendra at fullback. Weinke passed Danny Kanell for the school touchdown record (59) when he hit Bell for 2 touchdowns and threw another 58-yard score to Morgan. After the rout of the Terrapins, the Seminoles traveled to Miami, where they suffered their only regular-season loss, a 27-24 heartbreaker against the Hurricanes.

Win No. 310
Florida State 63, Duke 14
October 14, 2000
2000 Season: 6-1
Weinke had one of the best days a college quarterback could have as he established game, season, and career passing records. The senior quarterback threw for a school record 536 yards, surpassing the single-game passing mark that Bill Cappleman (who watched Weinke's performance from the stands at Doak Campbell) established in 1969. Weinke's offensive explosion also overtook Charlie Ward's total offense record of 529 yards. After the Blue Devils scored their first touchdown on an 84-yard punt return midway through the third quarter, Weinke came back with a 48-yard touchdown pass to Bell giving him the record. The throw was one of his 5 scoring passes on the game, giving him 66 career touchdown passes—a new ACC record. Former FSU first baseman Doug Mientkiewicz,

who had just won an Olympic gold medal, watched Weinke's performance from the sideline of the seventh-ranked Seminoles.

Win No. 311
Florida State 37, Virginia 3
October 21, 2000
2000 Season: 7-1
Bowden moved ahead of former Clemson coach Frank Howard into second place in all-time ACC coaching wins with his 67th conference victory. He pulled out the win in Tallahassee with the help of his defense, which held the Cavaliers to 33 yards rushing and 199 yards of total offense. The Seminoles, led by linebacker Brian Allen, who had an interception, sacked the Virginia quarterbacks 5 times while forcing 5 turnovers in the easy win. Minnis, who had four receptions for 131 yards, and McCray each scored 2 touchdowns. On defense, Virginia played a two-deep zone throughout the game that left the middle wide open for the tight ends. Ryan Sprague took advantage of the opening and had a career game with four receptions for 87 yards. Bowden had trouble with the inconsistency of his kickers all year, but against the Cavaliers, Chance Gwaltney hit all three extra points and connected on field goal attempts of 22, 36, and 25 yards.

Win No. 312
Florida State 58, North Carolina State 14
October 28, 2000
2000 Season: 8-1
The sixth-ranked Seminoles were in Raleigh against Bowden's friend and former longtime assistant coach, Chuck Amato. Bowden abandoned his passing attack in favor of a running plan and completely dominated the 21st-ranked Wolfpack. Minor ran for 129 yards and 2 touchdowns to lead the Seminoles, who rushed for 324 yards. The team rushing mark was a high for the season and the most in five years. Greg Jones provided Bowden with a glimpse of the future as the freshman running back ran for 78 yards and a touchdown on 7 carries. After being held scoreless in the first quarter, the Seminoles put up 27 unanswered points in the second quarter, capped off by Tay Cody's 52-yard interception return for a touchdown. Florida State then scored 31 unanswered points in the second half.

Win No. 313
Florida State 54, Clemson 7
November 4, 2000
2000 Season: 9-1
In Bowden Bowl II, the fourth-largest crowd in Doak Campbell history saw the senior Bowden clinch his ninth consecutive ACC championship with an offensive outburst that netted 250 yards rushing and 521 yards passing. While Minor had 102 yards rushing, Weinke completed 27-of-43 passes for 2 touchdowns. His crisp passing picked apart the 10th-ranked Tigers as the quarterback set several records in every quarter of the game. "That was the best performance of his whole career," said Minnis, his favorite target. In the first quarter, the Seminoles were pinned on their 2-yard line. Weinke responded by hitting

Chris Weinke and Bowden discuss the offensive strategy.

Minnis for a 98-yard touchdown after a beautiful play-action fake from his end zone. That completion was the longest touchdown pass in Florida State history, surpassing the 96-yard completion from Jimmy Jordan to Kurt Unglaub in Bowden's first year at FSU. By the end of the second quarter, Weinke passed Kanell to become the school's all-time leader with his 11th 300-yard passing game. In the third quarter, Weinke broke the school single-season passing record when he passed Thad Busby and ended the game with 3,490 yards for the season.

Win No. 314

Florida State 35, Wake Forest 6

November 11, 2000

2000 Season: 10-1

Bowden continued to move up the career coaching wins list. The victory over the Demon Deacons in Winston-Salem put him into fourth place—ahead of the legendary Pop Warner. Minnis caught 6 passes for 122 yards and 3 touchdowns. With the Seminoles leading 21-6 at the start of the fourth quarter, Anquan Boldin put the game out of reach with 2 touchdown receptions. Weinke, who threw 5 touchdowns, completed 23-of-36 passes for 324 yards. This was his 12th 300-yard game of his career, giving him the ACC record. The win by the Seminoles extended their NCAA record streak of 10-win seasons to 14.

Win No. 315

Florida State 30, Florida 7

November 18, 2000

Season: 11-1

Bowden—who with the win moved into third place in all-time victories ahead of the legendary Amos Alonzo Stagg—had little trouble finishing his ninth straight season without a home loss as his third-ranked Seminoles hammered the fourth-ranked Gators by the largest margin of victory over UF since 1977. No doubt Florida Governor Jeb Bush was impressed as he walked the sidelines. While Weinke threw for 353 yards and 3 touchdowns, his defensive teammates deserved much of the credit for the win. The Florida State defense, which came into the season finale ranked fifth in the nation, held the potent Florida offense to a season low of 315 yards. "It's about time we proved we could shut down a highly ranked offense," said Darnell Dockett, whose defense held the Gators to 37 yards on the ground. Only 10 minutes into the contest, Florida State had already given up seven points and 81 yards to the rival Gators. But the defense, with the score 7-7, righted itself and held the Gators scoreless for the rest of the contest. Steve Spurrier, forced to abandon the run, saw his quarterbacks (Jesse Palmer and Rex Grossman) self destruct with interceptions and incomplete passes. Cody had 2 pickoffs while free safety Chris Hope added another. Weinke, who threw 2 touchdowns to Minnis and another score to Bell, ended the game with 9,789 career yards to move him in front of Duke's Ben Bennett as the career passing leader for the ACC. The quarterback's most noted accomplishment, however, came when he was awarded the 2000 Heisman Trophy. Being selected as college football's top player was a fitting tribute to Weinke's career. Originally recruited in the class of 1990, he opted for a brief career in professional baseball before joining Bowden in 1997. Minnis, who had career highs with 8 receptions and 187 yards, ended a spectacular season in which he had 1,289 yards, second behind Ron Sellers on the FSU single-season receiving yardage list. Although the Seminoles moved up to second place in the BCS standings and received their third consecutive invitation to the national championship game, they came out on the short end of a 13-2 score against Oklahoma in the Orange Bowl.

Doak Campbell Stadium (2001) was selected by CBS Sportsline.com as one of the top 10 college football venues in 2003. The field will become Bobby Bowden Field when he retires.

YEAR THIRTY-SIX: THE 2001 SEASON (8-4)

Win No. 316

Florida State 55, Duke 13

September 1, 2001

2001 Season: 1-0

Coach Bowden had one of his youngest squads (including only 10 returning starters) in nearly two decades. Still, the Seminoles were ranked sixth in the nation and favorites to destroy the Blue Devils. Chris Rix, the first freshman ever to start at quarterback for a Bowden-coached team, was one of 12 new starters in the season opener at Duke. The young Seminoles—still trying to overcome the death of linebacker Devaughn Darling during practice seven months earlier—were able to overcome jitters and rookie mistakes to extend Duke's nation-leading losing streak. Duke punter Trey McDonald struggled throughout the game and provided the Seminoles with enough cushion to pull out a relatively easy victory. McDonald botched one snap that was recovered by Michael Boulware, brother of former FSU great Peter Boulware. The turnover set up a William McCray touchdown to give FSU a 10-6 second-quarter lead. On Duke's next possession, freshman Jerome Carter blocked McDonald's punt attempt and took it in for a 12-yard touchdown return. Kyler Hall, another true freshman, blocked yet another McDonald punt, which Gennaro Jackson recovered in the end zone to give FSU a 38-6 lead early in the third quarter.

Win No. 317

Florida State 29, Alabama-Birmingham 7

September 8, 2001

2001 Season: 2-0

The Seminoles relied on freshmen to lead the way for the second straight game. Xavier Beitia made 3 field goals, giving Bowden confidence that Beitia could be called upon at any time. Beitia proved his coach correct, hitting 13-of-14 field goal attempts in 2001. After his second field goal, Rix scored and made the highlight shows as he was flipped over after trying to hurdle a Blazer defender. His run put the Seminoles ahead 13-0 at halftime. During intermission, Bowden communicated with his new offensive coordinator (son Jeff Bowden) a desire to change the game plan to give Rix more freedom to scramble. The adjustment paid off early in the third quarter when Rix scrambled out of the pocket for a 16-yard first down that set up a 1-yard touchdown run by McCray. Rix led the team with 52 rushing yards, the first quarterback to do that at FSU since Charlie Ward in 1993. Remarkably for such a young team, FSU had no turnovers through two games.

Win No. 318

Florida State 48, Wake Forest 24

September 29, 2001

2001 Season: 3-1

Due to the World Trade Center attacks, the originally scheduled game against Georgia Tech was moved to the last game of the regular season. When football resumed, the Seminoles lost to North Carolina at Kenan Memorial Stadium for only the third ACC loss in 75 games. FSU dropped to No. 18, but rebounded with a strong first half against the visiting Demon Deacons, scoring on six straight drives. Rix had the best day of his young career by throwing for 345 yards, including touchdowns to Talman Gardner, Javon Walker, and B.J. Ward. Nick Maddox added 2 rushing touchdowns and 94 yards on the ground. Kendyll Pope intercepted 2 passes and had 10 tackles to lead FSU's defense.

Win No. 319

Florida State 43, Virginia 7

October 20, 2001

2001 Season: 4-2

After losing at home for the first time in 10 years with a setback to Miami, Bowden put the Seminoles through three exhausting practices in preparation for the game at Virginia. The effort didn't appear to pay off in the first half—the Seminoles could only build a 10-7 lead. But the rout was on early in the third quarter when McCray scored on a short run, Beitia hit a field goal, and Abdul Howard returned an interception 80 yards. The Seminoles put up an additional 17 unanswered points in the fourth quarter. Greg Jones had 107 yards rushing while Walker added 124 yards receiving. Bradley Jennings led the defense with 10 tackles. Bowden, who earlier in the week signed a lifetime contract that will pay him $2 million in total compensation per season, now ranked behind only the 323 wins of Bear Bryant and Joe Paterno. The only other coaches in Bowden's salary range at the time he agreed to the deal were Florida's Steve Spurrier and Oklahoma's Bob Stoops. The annual compensation was a far cry from the $4,200 he received at his first coaching position at South Georgia College.

Win No. 320
Florida State 52, Maryland 31
October 27, 2001
2001 Season: 5-2
With the defeat of the Terrapins, Bowden moved ahead of Glen "Pop" Warner to take sole possession of third place on the career wins list. The victory, however, appeared to be in doubt when Rix took a hard hit in the first quarter that put him on the bench. The Seminoles quickly fell behind 14-0 to the visiting Terrapins. But when team physicians Doug Henderson, Tom Haney, and Kris Stowers cleared Rix, he returned in a big way, throwing for 350 yards and 5 touchdowns. His performance began with 2 touchdown passes to Gardner. In-between those scores, Boulware, who tied Chris Hope with 3 interceptions on the season, picked off a pass and went 23 yards for his second touchdown on the year. Tied at 31 with a quarter remaining, Rix excelled by leading drives that ended with touchdown throws to Gardner (28 yards), Walker (22 yards), and Atrews Bell (31 yards).

Win No. 321
Florida State 41, Clemson 27
November 3, 2001
2001 Season: 6-2
While Clemson honored its 1981 national championship team, Bowden was in no mood for any celebrations by the Tigers or their coach, Tommy Bowden. Papa Bowden, who wore in 2001 a new wide-brimmed hat that Nike designed specifically for him to protect his face

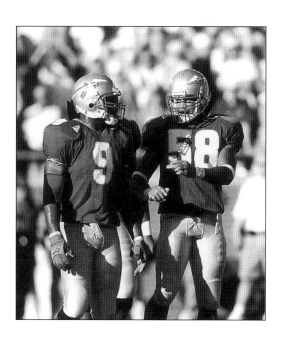

Kendyll Pope (9) and Michael Boulware (58) led the FSU defense in 2001.

from the sun, improved to 3-0 against his son with the impressive win in front of 85,000 at Memorial Stadium. Rix led the offense and his 369 passing yards and four touchdowns helped propel him to ACC rookie of the year honors. Walker and Jones also had career days. Walker caught 6 passes for 162 yards and 2 touchdowns while Jones rushed 17 times for 160 yards, including a 51-yard touchdown run. Jennings, Pope, Howard, Boulware, and Hope recorded double digits in tackles. Alonzo Jackson—who had 5 sacks on the season to lead the Seminoles—had 2 against the Tigers.

Win No. 322
Florida State 28, Georgia Tech 17
December 1, 2001
2001 Season: 7-4
Setbacks to North Carolina State and Florida had given the Seminoles back-to-back losses for the first time in 10 years. In Tallahassee against the Yellow Jackets, Rix led FSU to 3 unanswered touchdowns to start the second half. His first touchdown on an 8-yard quarterback keeper put the Seminoles permanently in the lead early in the third quarter. He then threw a touchdown to Walker for a 49-yard score and a 21-10 FSU lead. McCray finished the FSU scoring with a 2-yard touchdown run in the fourth quarter. Jerel Hudson (12 tackles) and Pope (10 stops) led the FSU defense while Darnell Dockett continued to dominate, setting a school record with 5 tackles for a loss. Dockett—an All-ACC selection—set the FSU single-season record with 22 tackles for a loss.

Win No. 323 (Gator Bowl)
Florida State 30, Virginia Tech 17
January 1, 2002
2001 Season: 8-4
The 24th-ranked Seminoles did not have far to go for the Gator Bowl at Alltel Stadium. Florida State, an underdog to the 15th-ranked Hokies, traveled to Jacksonville for a bowl game for the first time since 1985. Bowden, who won his 16th straight bowl game when his Seminoles were not playing for a national championship, guided his team with the help of strong performances from his special teams, defense, and the throw-and-catch combination of Rix and Walker. Although the season had been one of the most disappointing in the Bowden era, as the Seminoles failed to reach the 10-win plateau or add to their top-five finish record, Bowden knew that a win in the Gator Bowl would ease some of the pain. The game turned for the Seminoles with a blocked punt that set up the first score by the Seminoles. Down 3-0 with seven minutes remaining in the second quarter and the Florida State offense sputtering, Marcello Church squeezed past the Virginia Tech line to block a punt. Florida State then scored 10 unanswered points with a touchdown run by Rix and a field goal by Beitia to give the Seminoles a 10-3 halftime lead. Jones added a 5-yard touchdown run and Rix hit Walker for touchdown passes of 77 and 23 yards to secure the win. Walker's 194 receiving yards broke Fred Biletnikoff's Florida State bowl record. The victory for Bowden, who improved to 14-0 against the Hokies, gave the legendary coach 250 wins at FSU and a tie in career wins (323) with his coaching idol and early mentor, Bear Bryant.

After the Marching Chiefs play the theme from "The Good, The Bad, and The Ugly," the Seminoles gather around Bowden at the 20-yard line.

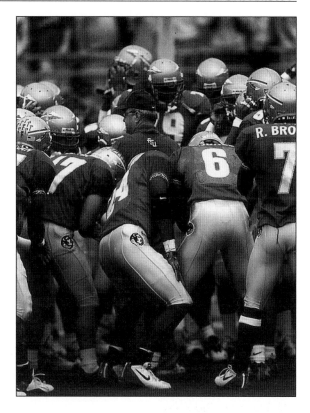

YEAR THIRTY-SEVEN: THE 2002 SEASON (9–5)

Win No. 324
Florida State 38, Iowa State 31
August 24, 2002
2002 Season: 1-0

As Bobby Bowden entered his 50th year as an assistant or head coach, he was tied in career wins with his coaching hero, Bear Bryant. Passing the legendary Alabama coach to take sole possession of second place on the career wins list proved to be a nail biter. "I really felt we lost," said Bowden after his third-ranked Seminoles pulled out a close win against the Cyclones in front of 55,000 spectators during the Eddie Robinson Classic at Arrowhead Stadium in Kansas City. In the end, it took a goal-line stand with four seconds remaining and Iowa State on the 1-yard line for Bowden to advance past Bryant. "It's a great honor," said Bowden, who was presented his first FSU game ball by co-captain Brett Williams. After Williams told Bowden that the game ball would probably mean a lot more to the coach 20 years down the road, Bowden responded, "Yeah, you all come out to the cemetery and remind me. I'll be underneath the grass." Against the Cyclones, the Seminoles took a commanding 24-0 lead at the beginning of the second quarter. But Iowa State fought back, outscoring FSU 31-14 and nearly pulling out the upset. Bowden's longtime defensive coordinator Mickey Andrews, who was forced to create a unique defensive strategy to contain Iowa State's Seneca Wallace on the final drive of the game, went with three down linemen, four linebackers, and four defensive backs. The adjustment worked; co-captain Jerel Hudson and Kendyll Pope filled their lanes and stopped a game-tying touchdown attempt by Wallace at the 1-yard line on the last play of the game.

Win No. 325
Florida State 40, Virginia 19
August 31, 2002
2002 Season: 2-0
Florida State, which received a pre-game pep talk by Warrick Dunn and Peter Boulware, came into the game having dropped to No. 5 in the polls. Virginia wanted to limit Chris Rix's effectiveness, so the Cavaliers dropped eight men into coverage for much of the game. While this did limit Rix (who failed to throw a touchdown for the first time in his career), it did provide an opportunity for FSU to use its running game. Florida State built a 23-0 halftime lead behind the strong running (76 yards) of Greg Jones. The 248-pounder, whom *ESPN The Magazine* said, "looked like Eddie George," ran for a career-high 173 yards and 2 touchdowns. The Seminoles—who built their lead to 33-0—rushed for 397 yards, the most since the 1995 season. Reserves played much of the second half in front of a home crowd of 79,000.

Greg Jones scored twice against Virginia.

Win No. 326

Florida State 37, Maryland 10

September 14, 2002

2002 Season: 3-0

In 2001, Florida State handed Maryland its only regular-season loss. But the Terrapins won conference bragging rights when they won the league title. Now, the Seminoles were determined to reclaim the crown that they had owned for nine straight seasons. "We want the ACC title back," said Rix in a postgame interview. In front of a sellout crowd at Byrd Stadium, the No. 5 Seminoles made their intentions clear by building a 30-0 first-half lead. Bowden relied on his quarterback and defense (which made sideline spectator Corey Simon proud) for the win. In the second quarter, Rix threw 2 touchdown passes and kept the ball for another score. Anquan Boldin, sidelined all of last year with a knee injury, proved to be the go-to receiver for the third consecutive game. He caught 5 crucial passes for 91 yards and 1 touchdown. Boldin finished the year by winning the Piccolo Award, given to the most courageous player in the ACC. The FSU defense dominated the game, especially in the first half where the Seminoles forced 6 turnovers.

Win No. 327

Florida State 48, Duke 17

September 21, 2002

2002 Season: 4-0

Florida State pounded the visiting Blue Devils with a strong passing game and a high-scoring second quarter. While the running game had been very effective in previous games, Florida State worked on its passing game against Duke. Most (404 yards) of Florida State's 510 yards of offense came through the air. The Seminoles, who struggled to get a field goal in the first quarter, scored on all three of their second-quarter possessions and went into halftime leading 24-3. In the second half, they built on their lead, eventually going ahead 45-3 as reserves occupied most positions on the field. All three quarterbacks (Rix, Adrian McPherson, and Fabian Walker) received plenty of playing time as Florida State went to its Kentucky Derby rotation. Bowden took a major hit when a Blue Devil ran into him on the sideline in the fourth quarter. "I don't believe I've been hit that hard since college," said Bowden. "I've seen head coaches get their legs broken." He added that his main concern about a leg injury is that it would "ruin my golf game."

Win No. 328

Florida State 48, Clemson 31

October 3, 2002

2002 Season: 5-1

A week earlier, Florida State's hopes for an undefeated season were dashed after a 26-20 rain-soaked, overtime loss at Louisville. The Seminoles had to quickly put the defeat behind them as the one-loss Tigers were in town for a Thursday-night game on ESPN. The fourth meeting between father and son was close throughout the first half with four lead changes. The Seminoles pulled ahead for good late in the second quarter. Jones had a spectacular night on the ground. The South Carolina native, who ran for 160 yards against

Chris Rix looks for an open receiver.

Clemson a year earlier, rushed for 165 yards and 3 scores on only 22 carries. Most impressive was his third touchdown of the night in which he broke eight tackles on his way to the end zone. Darnell Dockett, who has the words "Limited" and "Edition" tattooed down his arms, had 1 tackle for a loss to break the school record held by Ron Simmons. Dockett finished the year with a career total of 48 tackles for a loss. Bowden, who improved to 4-0 against Tommy, commented after the victory, "It's no fun when you whip your son. But I didn't tell him to get into coaching."

Win No. 329
Florida State 34, Wake Forest 21
November 2, 2002
2002 Season: 6-3
Florida State had not lost three games in a row since the 1980s. The Seminoles, after back-to-back losses to No. 1 Miami and No. 6 Notre Dame, took drastic measures to break the losing slump. In the boldest of moves, Bowden declared on the Monday before the game that McPherson would be his starting quarterback. Despite the adjustments, Wake Forest opened up a 14-0 first-quarter lead. But McPherson and Nick Maddox (who replaced Jones

after he was lost for the season with a knee injury) —and a defense that closed gaps that were wide open earlier in the game—methodically pulled FSU back into the game. Although FSU went into halftime behind (24-21) for the first time all season, momentum had clearly shifted. McPherson threw for 278 yards and 2 touchdowns and Maddox had 122 rushing yards as the visiting Seminoles beat the Demon Deacons for the 11th straight time.

Win No. 330
Florida State 21, Georgia Tech 13
November 9, 2002
2002 Season: 7-3
On Friday, Bowden turned 73 years old. On Saturday, his 17th-ranked Seminoles traveled to Atlanta, where they beat the Yellow Jackets to remain undefeated in the conference and keep their BCS hopes alive. But against Georgia Tech, an anemic offense needed to be bailed out by the defense. The offensive struggles were not unexpected, as replacements filled key positions. Although McPherson was not as effective as he had been in his first start, Maddox had 59 yards in the fourth quarter alone and ended the game tying his career best with 122 yards. But it was the 2 interceptions by Stanford Samuels that saved the day for the Seminoles. Samuels returned one of his interceptions 82 yards for a touchdown in the first quarter. His second interception, snared in the end zone with under 30 seconds on the clock, preserved the win for the Seminoles.

Alonzo Jackson spearheaded a dominant defense against North Carolina.

Win No. 331

Florida State 40, North Carolina 14

November 16, 2002

2002 Season: 8-3

The Seminoles celebrated homecoming with a 17-0 halftime lead and scored on four of their first five second-half possessions, securing their 10th ACC title with the defeat of the Tar Heels. Boldin provided the spark with 3 touchdown receptions. "Anquan is our playmaker," said Bowden. McPherson threw a career-high four touchdowns. The FSU defense returned to its dominant form by forcing 3 turnovers, recording 2 sacks, and knocking down 13 passes. In the regular season, the Seminoles recorded 16 sacks, led by Alonzo Jackson's 11 and Kevin Emanuel's 4. With the win over the Tar Heels, Bowden improved to 258-62-4 at Florida State.

Win No. 332

Florida State 31, Florida 14

November 30, 2002

2002 Season: 9-4

After a loss to North Carolina State the previous week, Bowden commented that the "tough" season could be salvaged with a win over the 11th-ranked Gators. Florida, which struggled early in the season under first-year head coach Ron Zook, was traveling to Doak Campbell with confidence and a four-game winning streak. Rix, in returning to the position he lost over a month earlier, rallied his Seminoles and quickly stifled any momentum the Gators brought with them. While his 194 yards of passing offense weren't gaudy statistics, his ability to avoid mistakes, run (83 yards), and lead long drives that resulted in points in every quarter made the difference. Both of Rix's touchdowns were to Boldin. Leon Washington, who started in place of the injured Maddox, added 134 yards on the ground on 26 carries. The Florida State defense kept Rex Grossman off rhythm throughout the game with numerous hurries, 2 sacks by Travis Johnson, and an interception by Pope that was returned for a touchdown early in the third quarter. Bowden, whose 22nd-ranked Seminoles had beaten the Gators for the fourth time in five years, improved to 16-12-1 against Florida. The next stop for Florida State was the Sugar Bowl, where the Seminoles lost to Georgia. Former Bowden assistant Mark Richt led the Bulldogs over his previous boss. "I have no desire to retire," Bowden announced after the bowl. "Now, I'm not God. I don't know when I'll leave this Earth, but as long as I'm healthy, I simply have no desire to retire." Bobby Bowden has no immediate plans to leave the game, and Seminole fans watch with anticipation as their coach—who turns 74 on November 8, 2003—continues to build upon his winning legacy.

Coach Bobby Bowden looks to the future.

PHOTO CREDITS

Every effort has been made to identify the photographer of each of the photographs used in this book.

Ross Obley
Front cover, back cover, pages 10, 64, 74, 92, 94, 95, 97, 98, 100, 102, 104, 109, 111, 112, 113, 116, 118, 120, 121, 123, 124, 127, 129, 130, 132, 133, 135, 136, 139, 141, 142, 143, 145, 146, 147, 148, 151, 152, 155, 157, 158, 161, 162, 164, 167, 169, 170, 172, 174, 177, 179, 181, 183, 184, 186, 187, and 189.

Florida State University Sports Information Department
Pages 54, 55, 57, 62, 63, 66, 68, 69, 71, 75, 79, 81, 82, 85, 86, 88, 90, 99, 106, 107, 114, and 122.

Samford University Archives
Pages 8, 11, 13, 15, 16, 18, 20, 21, 22, 23, 24, 26, 28, 29, and 30.

West Virginia University Sports Information Department
Pages 31, 32, 34, 35, 36, 37, 38, 39, 41, 42, 43, 44, 45, 47, 48, 49, 50, and 53.

Debbie Obley
Page 92.

"While Bobby Bowden is certainly one of college football's legends based on his wins and impact on the game, those are not his most admirable accomplishments. In my opinion, his impact on the lives of the players he has coached and the dramatic effect he has had on the growth of Florida State University as an ambassador are even more impressive than his victories and stature among college football immortals. Success never changed his priorities. His core values remained intact. That says it all about the man."

Dave Hart
Director of Athletics, Florida State University

AUTHOR AND PHOTOGRAPHER INFORMATION

Ray G. Schneider (center) teaches in the sport management department at Bowling Green State University. Schneider received his Ph.D. in sport management from Florida State University and has published numerous articles related to intercollegiate athletics in a variety of journals. An avid fan of all sports, Schneider has completed five marathons and earned letters in both baseball and basketball while an undergraduate at Central Michigan University. He lives in Maumee, Ohio, with his wife, Janet, and their son, Taylor (1).

Paul M. Pedersen (right) is a faculty member in the Rinker School of Business at Palm Beach Atlantic University (PBAU). Pedersen, who received his Ph.D. in sport management from FSU, holds degrees from PBAU, Emerson College, and the University of Central Florida. He has given 20 presentations at professional conferences and published over 15 sport management articles in national and international scholarly journals. He is also the author of *Build It and They Will Come: The Arrival of the Tampa Bay Devil Rays* and co-author of a book chapter in *The Business of Sport*. Pedersen lives in Stuart, Florida, with his wife, Jen, and their three children, Hallie (8), Zack (6), and Brock (2).

Ross P. Obley (left) is the chief investment officer for the Capital City Trust Company in Tallahassee, Florida. He received his MBA from Florida State University. Ross has photographed Florida State University athletics events for over 20 years and lives in Tallahassee, Florida, with his wife, Debbie.